When God Calls:
Listening, Hearing and
Responding

Dianne Sealy-Skerritt

Published by

MELROSE BOOKS

An Imprint of Melrose Press Limited
St Thomas Place, Ely
Cambridgeshire
CB7 4GG, UK
www.melrosebooks.co.uk

FIRST EDITION

Copyright © Dianne Sealy-Skerritt 2018

The Author asserts her moral right to
be identified as the author of this work

Cover designed by Melrose Books

ISBN   **978-1-912333-49-3 Hardback**
           978-1-912333-50-9 Paperback
           978-1-912333-51-6 epub
           978-1-912333-52-3 mobi

Printed and bound in Great Britain by:
CPI Group (UK) Ltd, Croydon, CR0 4YY

About the Author

Dianne Sealy-Skerritt is a retired Church of England officer and a contributing author to the Archbishop of York's bestselling book, *Hope Stories: 20 True Stories Changing Lives Today* (Sentamu, John; 2014; Darton Longham Todd Ltd). She was Equality and Diversity Officer for the Church of England (Diocese of Southwell and Nottingham) from 2007 until early 2017. As part of this role, she led the Rainbow Project for racial diversity and social justice for asylum-seekers, refugees and other socially marginalised groups. Dianne also has a professional background in management development consultancy, staff development and training, social work, adoption and fostering. She was Nottinghamshire County Council's first African-Caribbean senior social worker. In her freelance management consultancy role, her customers included Nottinghamshire Constabulary with whom she worked on issues arising from the Stephen Lawrence Inquiry. She has served on the board of a number of local and national organisations to promote equality and social justice. Dianne pioneered the Church of England's relationship with the Gypsy Roma Traveller Communities and was instrumental in promoting its collaboration with Pentecostal Majority

Black-led Churches. She also represented the Diocese on the **Changing Attitudes Group** to promote the rights of Lesbians, Gay, Bisexual, Transgendered and Intersexual people.

Dedicated to two very special women:

Ms Claudia Webbe, a daughter by love,
who is living God's call daily

The late Dr Janet Hamilton – a beloved friend and colleague
who fought tirelessly for racial equality and justice for
women until the end of her life.

CONTENTS

Foreword: Reverend Christopher Harrison ix

Acknowledgements xii

Introduction xv

Chapter One   Making Sense of God,
                  Purpose and Calling....................................1

Chapter Two   Made for a Calling 23

Chapter Three Who God Calls –
                   Lessons From Biblical Call Stories...........48

Chapter Four   Who God Calls –
                   Lessons From Modern Call Stories..........77

Chapter Five   Hearing God's Call 113

Chapter Six   Ten Barriers to Hearing God's Voice......141

Chapter Seven Calling and Resilience 171

Epilogue   Don't Run Away When God Calls 202

References 214

Foreword

The word 'vocation' has traditionally been used by the Church to describe a calling to ordination or to the monastic life. In this book, however, Dianne Sealy-Skerritt shows how the sense of being called by God is fundamental to what it means to be human, and is not to be restricted to a privileged few. She demonstrates how the discovery of a person's true calling can lead to a wonderful renewal of purpose, to a new confidence that life has meaning, and to the blessedness that results from being committed to following the ways of God.

Dianne brings to her writing the fruits of several decades of working with people from a wide range of backgrounds to promote equality and social justice. Her profound belief in a God who loves and cares for each individual, whatever their origin or place in society, shines through the pages of this book. She shows how a calling from God can emerge from contexts that might seem surprising or unexpected, which indicates how dangerous it is to make hasty judgements regarding vocations that might at first sight seem unconventional. She also reminds us that calling is more than paid work. Our calling embraces our whole being and how we use our gifts to respond to the needs of others.

I first came to know Dianne through my role as vicar of the churches of All Saints, St Mary and St Peter, Nottingham. It so happens that the dedication of each of these churches helps us to understand something of what it means to be called by God. The Blessed Virgin Mary, a teenage girl chosen to bear God's Son, is one of the key examples in the Bible of humility and obedience to the will of God. St Peter was called by Jesus to lead the early Church in spite of all his weaknesses and failings, showing us also the renewing power of God's forgiveness and patience.

It is when the Church commemorates All Saints' Day, however, that we are reminded of the millions of people through the centuries who have been called to lives of holiness and devotion to God, most of whom have now been largely forgotten by the world. A deep awareness that God's kingdom of love, justice and peace will result from the lives of the millions of God's saints, not just of the few, is evident throughout this book. This contributes powerfully to the message of hope that Dianne offers to us all, which is especially important at a time in world history that seems increasingly perilous.

Perhaps you have given up hope of finding meaning or purpose in life. Maybe you have lost the ability to believe in yourself and your desires; or you have become convinced, from what others have told you, that you are no value to anyone. If so, this book will be a source of encouragement and practical guidance to you. But it will also be an inspiration to all who are seeking to go beyond what is merely safe and comfortable, and who are willing to venture into new and unpredictable territory, guided by the unfailing love of God.

Rev Christopher Harrison
Rector of St Peter and All Saints, Nottingham

Acknowledgements

This book is the result of a divine assignment. I resisted putting fingers to keyboard for a long time as I had no prior experience of writing and publishing books. After much prayer and meditation, I had an unexpected meeting with a stranger (Dr Courtney Smith, author of the very inspirational book, *The Wonderful You: Find Your Purpose and Live the Life of Your Dreams Now*) at a meeting normally reserved for women. He generously offered to guide me through the whole publishing process and provide me with research, editorial and technical support. I owe Dr Smith a huge debt of gratitude as this book would not have been possible *at this point in time* without the benefit of his expertise and constant encouragement. I am also grateful to Rachel Hutchinson and the rest of the team at Melrose Publishers for their belief in the book and for working with me in partnership and with great professionalism to turn my vision into reality.

I would also like to convey heartfelt thanks to Reverend Christopher Harrison for writing the foreword and for reviewing sample chapters from the book. The book has been much improved as a result of his very helpful and insightful feedback and support. In addition, throughout my call, he has been a constant source of support and encouragement. My debt to those who responded to my research questionnaire and allowed me to share their call stories is enormous. I would like to say a huge thank you to Reverend Sonia Barron, Mrs Deloris Hall, Dr Claire Jenkins, Mr Freddie Kofi and Dr Garrick Wilson. Chapter four would not have been possible without their contributions. Although not helping directly with the production of the book, my family and friends offered a great deal of moral support and kept me going. My love and thanks go to my children, grandchildren, great grandchildren, godchildren and their loved ones. Thanks a million to Yemisi Adegun, Veronica Bell, Nina Branch, Lilleth Clarke, Elisabeth Crouch, Kristina Farnum, Margo Fenty-Moore, Louis Francis, Faith Gakanje-Ajala, Dr Elizabeth Henry, Caroline Jarvis, Stefan Hall, Carl Matthews, Leith Rayside, Phyllis Richardson, Deborah Simon, Claudia Webbe, Elaine White and Juanita Wood.

I would also like to acknowledge the many organisations, groups and people whom I have worked with as part of my call. Many of them have enabled my call and were particularly supportive during periods of professional and personal setbacks. Understandably, they are too numerous to mention individually, and I hope no one will be offended if their name is omitted. I am particularly grateful to the members of The Women of Faith Nottingham and the staff at the Diocese of Southwell and Nottingham who have supported me during my tenure at the Diocese.

The following individuals have made a positive and lasting impact on my call journey and I would like to extend my deepest thanks to them: Archbishop John Sentamu, Dr Bishop Joe Aldred, Bishop Paul Butler, Bishop George Cassidy, Bishop Ruth Worsley, Reverend Graham Burton, The Very Reverend John Guille, Reverend Alan Payne, Reverend Karen Rooms, Reverend Arlington Trotman, Sharon Bravo, Eleanor Dunleavy, Catriona Gundlach, Amdani Juma, Celia Kellett, Frazer McNish, Sara Palacios Arapiles, Julian Singh, Dorothy Tatem, Paddy Tipping and Jane Wyles. I am also deeply grateful to all the wonderful people who have contributed to the annual Racial Justice Weekends (especially my granddaughter, Chanae Skerritt) which I led and those who were allied to my work at The Rainbow Project.

Introduction

"For I know the plans I have for you, declares the Lord, plans to prosper you and not to harm you, plans to give you hope and a future."   Jeremiah 29:11

Nothing is more important than God's calling on our life.[1] A calling is a unique and personal assignment given to us by God for His greater purpose. It encompasses our whole being and doing. Contrary to popular belief, it is not limited to church ministry or to what we do in a workplace setting. Our work or vocation is only one aspect of our call. What we do outside of church or the workplace may be the most important part of God's call on our life. First and foremost, we are called to develop a loving and trusting relationship with God. Our call also includes our relationship with our family and with those who we serve. It is not a single task. God has defined a unique path for each of us to follow, where we will experience deep self-fulfilment, love, joy, meaning and satisfaction.

God's call on our lives is universal. No one is excluded on grounds of their age, race, culture, gender, faith, marital status, health status, disability, sexual orientation, socio-economic

---

1 Although the book sometimes refers to God in the masculine gender, please note that this is done for mere convenience to avoid over-repeating the word God. God is not a physical or human entity – neither a "he" or a "she".

status or any other 'questionnaire' category. God relies on each individual to do His work in the world. As Archbishop Desmond Tutu rightly says, *"Without us, God has no eyes; without us, God has no ears; without us, God has no arms or hands"*. He is a God of diversity and equality. Each person has a unique role to play in His divine plan and is equal in His eyes. We are God's partners in the world. God expects us to use our gifts to serve others, wherever there is a need. We are here to become His representative in the world and to make our unique contribution to His divine plan. We cannot accomplish this role if we bury our gifts or sleep-walk through life.

To know God's call for our life, we need to acknowledge His existence, develop a relationship, and respond with obedience when He speaks to us. Our call will be revealed to us if we seek Him earnestly.

I was blessed to know my call from my childhood years. I knew it was about being a champion and advocate for justice and equality, even though I was not sure where and how this would play out in practice. Through my close relationship with God, I later realised that He was using all the events, circumstances, personal experiences and people in my life to prepare me for this call. I was placed in jobs and situations where I saw first-hand how discrimination, injustice and exclusion could be entrenched in institutions where one would least expect to find such practices. While equality and diversity policies existed on paper in some of the organisations where I served, this was purely to comply with legislations and the requirements of the Human Resources department. The policies were never implemented, and the culture did not hold leaders and managers to account. Instead it seems as if they were designed to perpetuate the status quo and provide senior management with a shield to counter any allegations of unfair practices.

As a result of God's call on my life, I was able to expose discriminatory practices and champion the cause of those who were socially excluded and marginalised in society. God gave me the passion, strength and support to fight and win many battles against the odds to bring them justice. I ruffled many feathers and faced huge opposition during the course of my call, but remained obedient to God. A call is never a smooth journey. You can expect to face major challenges, but God will always be present with you in such times. Before launching us into our calling, He always prepares the way and sustains us during the whole journey. In the case of my own call, I go where God leads me with total obedience and unflappable courage. I have been labelled a 'loose cannon' and other derogatory terms by senior managers for living out my call. I have faced covert racism and bullying but, to their disgust, such acts only served to increase my resolve to fulfil my call.

A call from God is a continuous, cradle to grave experience. It is not finished until we reach the end of our life. It is only then that we are no longer able to use our gifts to serve others. Writing this book is also part of my call. God has given me a message to share with my readers. The message is challenging and hard-hitting in places, but I hope it will be taken in good faith.

I have written this book for the benefit of everyone. The book offers guidance to enable people of all age groups and backgrounds to recognise and fulfil their calling. It includes a range of inspirational case studies from the Bible and other sources on how people heard and pursue their call from God. The lessons from these call stories are analysed to provide a clear road-map about the nature of God's call and how to navigate obstacles along the way. These include insights from my own call journey to date. The book will help you to walk more closely with God so that you too can find your call and live the life that God intended for you. It shatters the myth that calling is something that only happened in Biblical times and that it is reserved for special people.

As a practical guidebook, it addresses key questions such as:

- What does it mean to be called by God?
- How do we find our call?
- Who does God call?
- How does God call us?
- How do we distinguish God's voice from other voices?
- How should we respond when God calls?
- How does God prepare us for our calling?
- What are the barriers to hearing God's voice?
- How can we overcome fear and the tendency to resist our call?
- How can we build our resilience and stay focused on our call in times of adversity?

STRUCTURE

The book is organised into eight chapters. Chapter One explains what is meant by 'calling' and 'purpose'. As God means different things to different people, this opening chapter also discusses different notions and images of God.

Chapter Two explains why God made us and how He equips us for our call. It provides guidance to help readers to identify what God is calling them to do.

Chapters Three and Four discuss who God calls. Using a wide range of call stories from the Bible and real-world people from my community, I demonstrate that God calls everyone to serve His purpose. I also discuss the practical lessons from these call stories.

Chapter Five is devoted to how to hear God's call. It discusses the different ways God speaks to us and highlights the importance of obedience and courage in following His call. Guidance is offered on how to distinguish between God's voice and other voices.

Chapter Six examines barriers to hearing God's call. It also provides guidance on how to become better listeners.

Chapter Seven offers tips on how to build resilience to sustain us as we pursue our call. A call journey is never a smooth process. We cannot fulfil our call in our comfort zone. Expect to encounter mountains and valleys along the way. This chapter provides practical tools that you can use to navigate your call with confidence and courage in times of turmoil.

The Epilogue concludes with further reflections on

calling and the reality of a living, active and benevolent God. Readers are encouraged to define God for themselves and develop their own personal relationship with God. This chapter also reinforces the main message of this book – i.e. God calls everyone and never gives up on us even when we try to run away from our call (i.e. the 'Jonah Complex').

AUDIENCE

The book is written for a *universal* audience. I have made special efforts to tailor the material and language to readers of all age groups, faiths, denominations, creeds and cultural backgrounds. It will benefit anyone who wants to develop their spiritual awareness, build their resilience, fulfil their purpose and calling, and live a more meaningful and successful life. It will also appeal to churchgoers, church leaders and managers, minority groups, advocates for social justice, employers, professionals and anyone who wants to understand their call and have a meaningful relationship with God.

Although falling within the genre of spirituality, it will also be of practical value to those who are drawn to personal development and self-help books. If you have ever wondered why you are here and what is the purpose of life, this is just the book for you. True and lasting change has to come from *within* us when the penny drops, and this book will help you to do just that.

UNIQUE FEATURES

The book is distinguished from other titles on the subject of calling by its emphasis on practical guidance drawn from my lived experience. I have also had the benefit of working in the Church of England on equality, diversity and justice issues. The book boldly addresses how failure to *listen*, *hear* and *respond* to God's call can make it difficult for us to realise our potential and live the life we were created to have. There are also end–of–chapter discussion questions, designed to encourage readers to think more deeply about the issues and personally engage with the material.

Whatever stage you are at in your call journey, I hope this book will help you to identify your call and inspire you to pursue it with courage and total obedience to God. None of us is here by accident. We are all uniquely made in God's image and placed here as part of His divine plan to serve the world's needs. Use this book to guide you through your call and make a positive difference in the world.

Dianne Sealy-Skerritt
Nottingham, United Kingdom

Chapter One

Making Sense of God, Purpose and Calling

This chapter sets out the framework for understanding this book. It discusses the three key terms that are woven through the text – 'God', 'purpose' and 'calling'. As these words mean different things to different people, I will begin with some definitions and state my own perspective. Not everyone believes in God's existence or that God has a purpose for creating us. Your image and ideas of God have huge implications for your relationship with God and how you live your daily life. It is hard to hear God's call if you do not believe in a God who is real and active in the world. By the end of this chapter, you will be able to make an informed decision on God's existence and your role on earth.

THE REALITY OF GOD

> *"The fool said in his heart, there is no God."*
>
> Psalm 14:1

Nietzsche is credited with the saying that God is dead, but news of the Almighty's demise may have been greatly exaggerated. This book makes the bold claim that God is active and real in the universe, and that we all have a call and purpose, given to us by God, whether or not we are aware of it. Archbishop Desmond Tutu reminds us, *"Without us, God has no eyes; without us, God has no ears; without us, God has no arms or hands. God relies on us."* (Tutu, D., *God is Not a Christian*, p.xii).

The best place to begin this journey is with a discussion of what we mean when we talk about God. Before we can hear and respond to God's call, we need to accept the reality of God and trust in God's voice. The word conjures different images and meaning for everyone. What we believe about God is usually shaped by our childhood experiences and the significant people in our life.

God is not an old white man sitting above the clouds pronouncing judgements on those who are unfaithful to him. God is neither male nor female.

In my own case, my portrayal of God was heavily influenced by my grandparents (especially my grandmother), godparents, Sunday school teachers, primary school and secondary school (Girls' Foundation High School) teachers. I was introduced to church from a very young age whilst growing up in Barbados. I was christened in the Methodist Church at eight weeks old. I later attended Sunday school at an Anglican Church and was brought up to conform to our family's Anglican tradition. My grandfather was the headmaster of the Good Shepherd Anglican School and a lay-preacher for the Good Shepherd Church. By age 13, I made my own decision and began to attend a Catholic Church. I was attracted to their use of incense, the use of holy water, the use of Latin during mass and the other rituals. After much soul searching, in 2001, I was baptised in a Pentecostal Church. Since then I have come to the realisation that God can be found everywhere. I now feel I have the spiritual freedom to attend any church and worship God at all times. God should be worshipped everywhere and at all times, not just when we are in church.

I was taught to see God as an old man living beyond the clouds. God was portrayed to me as someone with the physical characteristics of Santa Claus – male, white, blue eyes, blond hair, and long white beard, someone who loves us and would grant us the things on our wish-list if we were 'good'. Nearly every household, including ours, had a photograph of a blue-eyed, long haired young man dressed in a white robe and sandals hung in a prominent location in their living room. I was told God would punish me and ignore my prayers if I did not keep all His commandments and act 'godly' at all times. Acting 'godly' went beyond complying with moral codes. Church attendance on Sundays was obligatory, as well as practicing the religious rituals.

Even the clothes we wore to church mattered. We were expected to adorn ourselves with our best clothes for Sunday worship. I can remember my immaculately polished shoes which were usually cleaned and polished by my grandfather, white socks, knee-length dress and my beautiful hats. My grandmother believed cleanliness was a part of godliness and God expected the best of what we have.

My image of God changed as I matured over the years. I devoted countless hours trying to understand the God depicted in the Bible and other sacred books such as the *Bhagavad Gita, Quran,* Vedas, *Husia,* and the *Buddhist Sutras.* I challenged almost everything I was told about God in light of my reading of these sacred books and my experience. When the penny dropped, I had a number of startling revelations.

First, I realised that God is not a physical entity living above the clouds. Since God is not a physical being, it is not meaningful to refer to God as male or female.

Second, God does not fall into any ethnic category. God is neither black, white, Asian or any of the ethnic categories we often see on questionnaires.

Third, God certainly does not live above the clouds. God is everywhere – within us, above us, below us, around us, beyond time and space. God is in all these places at the same time. We experience the presence and call of God in our life each day without even being aware of it. We experience it in the emotions we feel, the people we meet, the thoughts we think and the experiences we have.

Fourth, God is for all and is accessible by anyone. God does not just exist for Christians or a chosen group. God existed before religions were invented. Everyone is created in God's image and likeness. We are all of equal value in the sight of God, regardless of our faith, gender, nationality, ethnicity, disability, physical and mental condition, sexual orientation, personal preferences, socio-economic position or marital status. No one group or religion can claim God as 'our God'. Everyone has equal access to God.

Fifth, God can be known personally by everyone through prayer and faithful worship. That is partly what it means to be made in God's image and likeness. Every one of us is of God – we are 'Godlike'. Although God is not a physical entity, we can develop a more intimate and personal relationship with God by picturing God as a being with similar characteristics to ourselves. We are all God's children, so we should feel free to share God's characteristics.

This is the reason why God is personified in different cultural and religious traditions. God is personified as Caucasian in Christianity, 'Asian' in Islam, Jewish in Judaism, Chinese in Taoism, and 'African-Caribbean' in Rastafarianism and in some Pentecostal majority black-led churches. Every image of God is valid as it is a reflection of how each individual perceives the Reality of God. In the same way as we have a multiplicity of languages to express a thought or idea, there is no single way to express our image of God. Each language is of equal validity. Seeing God as a 'Christian' or 'Muslim' is like thinking that English or Arabic is the only valid language for speaking.

Sixth, God wants everyone to lead a fulfilling and prosperous life. God is a God of love, peace and justice. In subsequent chapters, I will demonstrate how each of us is called by God to live out these values and to serve others.

Remember, personification of God does not mean that God is a person with a literal physical form. If it helps you to connect more meaningfully with God, personification is a good practice. My own personal preference is to see God in the same way I see the air I breathe, rather than any form of personification. I know the air exists, even though I cannot see or touch it. Whilst I cannot see or touch it, I can feel it. When the wind blows it, I can see trees swaying and other objects moving. The air is essential to life. I cannot exist without it and I cannot exist without God. The fact that we cannot see or touch God does not make God non-existent or meaningless.

I see God as loving, merciful, forgiving, faithful, life-giving, and readily available in good and bad times. I also believe that, whether or not we are aware of it, God's image is imprinted in our nature. Our conscience serves as the voice of God. God's standards are programmed in our hearts. We instinctively know the difference between right and wrong. We know we are connected to each other and are created from the same Source. Young children show these innate qualities of morality, fairness, justice, love and all the things we associate with 'God-consciousness'. We often see children offering to help us with our chores, picking up dropped items, opening doors for others, and interrupting play to acknowledge others. Selfless acts of this kind are not the result of social conditioning.

We may choose to ignore what our conscience directs us to do but this does not mean it does not exist. It is the God-force within us that leads people naturally to help others in times of disasters. Some even risk their own life to save others. In a very fascinating book, *The God Gene*, Dean Hamer argues that our genetic structure includes a 'God gene' that predisposes us to spirituality. We are wired to know God and develop a personal relationship with God.

Dr Justin Barrett, a senior researcher at the Centre for Anthropology and Mind at the University of Oxford, has also concluded that children are 'born believers' in God and that this is not the result of any form of indoctrination or programming. He reported evidence from anthropologists which found that even in cultures where religious teachings are withheld from children, children still held a belief in God and know the difference between man-made objects and the things that are made by God (*see Born Believers: The Science of Children's Religious Belief*, Simon & Schuster, 2012).

There is a wide spectrum of other views about God. The images offered in these depictions of God tend to be more abstract and impersonal. These depict God as:

- Inner Self, Intuition, and Inner Knowing;
- Existence, Life, Breath and Reality itself;
- Love, Purity, Innocence and Justice;
- The Spirit which is present within us and every living thing;
- The Force which lies behind the order, beauty and symmetry in nature;
- Nature in all its manifestations (God is reflected in the trees, the oceans, the air we breathe and everything in nature);
- The Source of creation and everything within and beyond the cosmos;
- The Creator and Ruler of the universe and everything within it;
- A Higher Power or a Cosmic Force that created the world but does not actively intervene within it;
- A Higher Power, human-like, that actively and personally interacts with everyone through prayer and other means of communication; and
- The Supreme Being – a Being above all other beings. Paul Tillich goes further and describes God as 'Being itself', the source of all being, or the 'Ground of being itself'.

Words are a feeble attempt to describe the awe-inspiring and mysterious nature of God. Metaphors are often used in sacred texts to provide a more concrete glimpse of whom and what God is. The Bible alone contains several hundred metaphors to talk about God. God is described as Father, Mother, Shepherd, Spirit, Energy, Deliverer, Rock, King, Great Physician, Light of the World, The Way, The Truth and the Life, The Vine, The Bread of Life, The All, The One, The Creator, The Universal Mind, Consciousness, etc. Isaiah compared God to a Father and a Potter:

> *"But now, O Lord, You are our Father, we are the clay,*
> *and You our potter; And all of us are the work of Your*
> *hand"*   Isaiah 64:8

Although instructive, none of these images is powerful enough to adequately describe God. Benjamin Myers summarises this point well when he wrote: *"God is too full, too communicative, too bright and piercing"* to be understood with our finite minds. Some people see God as a single entity or what theologians term 'monotheism'. This is the case in Christianity, Judaism and Islam.

Others believe in the existence of multiple gods. In Greek mythology, 'polytheism' or a belief in many Gods was widely practiced. In Hinduism, for example, Braham manifests itself in thousands of Gods. For most Christian faiths, there is also the doctrine of the 'Trinity'. This states that there is only one God, but this God exists in three Divine Beings – God the Father, God the Son and God the Holy Spirit. All three are equal and have the same attributes, which I will describe in the next section. People often get confused with this teaching. It does not mean there are three separate Gods in Christianity as claimed, for example, by the Jehovah's Witnesses. It means the Father is God, the Son is God and the Holy Spirit is God. The Father is not the Son, the Son is not the Spirit and the Spirit is not the Father. They are three Divine Persons in one God – not three parts or pieces of God. An intuitive way to think of this is to think of someone who is a father, a son and a husband at one and the same time. Yet they are only one person.

In stark contrast, there are also those who question the existence of God. People in this category are usually labelled 'atheists' and 'agnostics'. Atheists deny the existence of God altogether while agnostics are sceptical about the existence of God as this is difficult to prove or disprove. Both agnostics and atheists stand apart from the 'theists' – the believers in God's existence. Atheists dismiss belief in God as superstition borne out of ignorance. To some, God is simply a security blanket for those who are overwhelmed by problems and setbacks. The well-known atheist, Richard Dawkins, sees belief in a God as a type of mental illness. I will consider the evidence for and against God in the final chapter of this book.

FOOD FOR THOUGHT: FOUR VIEWS OF GOD?

Research undertaken by Professors Paul Froese and Christopher Bader at Baylor University reports that Americans have four notions of God:

- Authoritarian God (a deity of divine judgement);
- Benevolent God (a deity which is loving and non-judgemental);
- Critical God (a deity of delayed judgement and little active engagement with the world); and
- Distant God (a deity who created the world but who is not actively involved in running it).

Source: Paul Frose and Christopher Bader, *America's Four Gods: What We Say About God – And What That Says About Us,* Oxford University Press, 2015.

What is your view of God?

GOD'S ATTRIBUTES

Now that you have given thought to what God means to you, let us consider God's attributes. Our awareness of God's attributes will help us to understand God and respond to His call in our lives. Sacred texts like the Bible and Quran emphasise God's 'omnipresence', 'omniscience', 'omnipotence', 'omnibenevolence', 'immutability' and 'sovereignty'. These are £1 million words beyond many people's comprehension. They are not everyday words, but they are the words commonly used to describe God's core attributes. These attributes are often dismissed by atheists, agnostics and people who believe in pagan, false gods. Let us consider the meaning of these terms more closely. The prefix 'omni' is just another way of saying 'all' or 'without limits'.

'Omnipresence' means God is present everywhere and in everything at the same time. God is not limited by time or space. King Solomon prayed:

> *"The heavens, even the highest heaven, cannot contain you. How much less this temple I have built!"*
>
> 1 Kings 8:27

'Omniscience' means God knows everything, being the Creator of knowledge and everything there is to know. God knew us before we were born and even the number of strands of hair we possess.

> *"Before a word is on my tongue you know it completely, O Lord."*   Psalms 139:4

God knows our thoughts, deeds, innermost desires and even our destiny. Our needs are known and understood by God, from whom nothing is hidden (Job 34:21–23). God knows every star by name (Psalms 147:4). We are talking about an almost countless number of stars. The Milky Way galaxy alone has some 200 billion stars and scientists tell us there are at least another 100 billion galaxies.

'Omnipotence' means God's power is limitless. God is able to do anything, and has a supreme power which was clearly seen at the time of creation, as shown by the words from God, *"Let there be light"* (Genesis 1:3), which were instantly fulfilled. Job wrote:

> *"I know that you can do all things; no plan of yours can be thwarted."*   Job 42:2

'Omnibenevolence' means God is perfectly moral and just, all-good, fully merciful, and all-loving. Christians believe that it is because of God's unconditional and infinite love, shown through the sacrifice of Jesus on the cross, that humanity is able to have the right relationship with God.

> *"But God demonstrates His own love for us in this: While we were still sinners, Christ died for us."*
> Romans 5:8

'Immutability' means God does not change. God is eternal, does not exist within time, and cannot change to become better or worse, because God is all-perfect. The unchanging and unchangeable nature of God is reflected throughout the Bible:

> *"I the Lord do not change"*   Malachi 3:6

and that often quoted verse in Hebrews 13:8:

"Jesus Christ is the same yesterday, today and forever".

A natural consequence of the attributes discussed above is God's sovereignty.

'Sovereignty' means God:

- controls and rules the entire universe;
- is at work in our lives and in everything that happens in the universe;
- does what needs to be done for the greater purpose; and
- has the power and knowledge to do anything that needs to be done.

Only a God with these attributes could create a universe and an earth as complex as the one we inhabit. The Psalmist writes,

"The heavens declare the glory of God; the skies proclaim the work of his hands."   Psalms 19:1

Some people continue to suppress the truth about God's existence and miraculous creation. In the Epilogue, I will provide incontrovertible evidence from science and other sources to substantiate my belief in a living and active God with the attributes discussed above.

PURPOSE AND CALLING

"The two most important days in your life are the day you are born and the day you find out why." Mark Twain

As we can see, therefore, so much of what we observe in the universe suggests that it is purposely designed for God's purpose. There is a purpose for everything God created. Purpose is about why something or someone exists. The *Merriam Webster's Dictionary* explains it as follows: *"[Purpose is] the reason for which something exists or is done, made, or used"*. It is *"an intended or desired result; end; aim; goal."*

Although related to calling, purpose is different from 'calling'. The *Merriam Webster's Dictionary* defines Calling as *"a strong inner impulse toward a particular course of action especially when accompanied by conviction of divine influence; the vocation or profession in which one customarily engages."* Your calling is what you are called to do – the set of assignments you are motivated to carry out to meet people's needs. Purpose may be viewed as the *end* to be attained while calling is the *means* to get to the end.

This may be explained by way of an analogy. For a charitable organisation working with disadvantaged groups in poorer parts of the world, its purpose may be to make the world a better place by reducing poverty and enhancing people's wellbeing. In pursuit of this end, the management team and staff are called to play different roles, drawing on their particular gifts and what they are passionate about. Some may be called to perform roles such as fund-raising, budgeting, communication, organising and running events, developing web-pages, managing people, dealing with the media, transportation, logistics management, governance, reporting, accountability, etc. The success of the organisation would depend on everyone working as part of a cohesive team with goals that are aligned to the overall purpose of the organisation. Each is called to make a distinctive contribution to fulfil the desired outcome. In putting the team together, we need to acknowledge the diversity of God's creation and the unique and distinctive contribution that each person can bring to the organisation.

Many people live their life without any clear sense of their purpose or calling. It is no wonder they lead lives that are meaningless and unfulfilling. If we reject God's existence, it follows that we will end up living a rudderless life. We would naturally fail to see the bigger picture for our life. We would not be aware of the master plan for our life from our designer. To know the purpose of anything, we need to find out from the designer or read the 'instruction manual'. For Christians, the Bible serves as the Instruction Manual for God's plan for human life. Going through life without a good idea of your life purpose and calling is like walking through a strange wooded forest without a compass.

The Bible provides ample clues about God's purpose for our lives. First and foremost, we were created to do good deeds to bring honour and glory to God. The Apostle Saint Paul writes:

"We are God's workmanship, created in Christ Jesus to do good works, which God prepared in advance for us to do"
                                                        Ephesians 2:10

God has given each created being a specific set of assignments to perform while we are on earth. Each of us has a vital role to play in God's eternal plan, which no one else can play. We are here to honour God's plan for our life, to heed His call and bring Him glory.

Our life purpose should be about God's plan, not ours. Giving glory to God is about reflecting His light in the world and exposing His nature in all our interactions with others. God's essence is love and everything we do in the world should be motivated by love and should reflect God's love. Glorifying God is also about using the gifts which He gives us to serve others. We displease God when we hide our talents and fail to show up in the world, whether due to fear or self-limiting beliefs from the way we are socially conditioned. God expects us to shine our light and be the best version of ourselves. We also bring glory to God when we are obedient to His call and follow His instructions.

By living our lives in alignment with God's purpose, we will find meaning and fulfilment. In contrast, our lives will feel empty and meaningless if we indulge in self-gratification and leave God out of the picture. King Solomon made this mistake and regretted it bitterly towards the end of his life. He was the richest and greatest person of his era. He had wealth, pleasure, wisdom, and fame without measure. He ultimately realised his mistake, however, and this realisation is described in the Book of Ecclesiastes:

"Then I looked on all the works that my hands had wrought, and on the labour that I had laboured to do: and behold, all was vanity and vexation of spirit, and there was no profit under the sun."   Ecclesiastes 2:11

In despair, Solomon cried out:

"Therefore I hated life; because the work that is wrought under the sun is grievous unto me: for all is vanity and vexation of spirit."   Ecclesiastes 2:17

Today we see people making the same mistake all over the world and, like Solomon, hating life. In spite of their wealth and status, many resort to psychics, superstition, drugs, and other types of addictive behaviours in their quest to find meaning and fulfilment. Some even harm themselves and end their own life.

Lasting happiness and fulfilment come from living in alignment with the purpose God has for your life and staying obedient to His call. We need to learn to hear God's call and live it out in all our daily activities. This does not just include your work or vocational activities. It includes your recreational activities, your relationships and everything you do.

Each time you feel a burning inner impulse toward a particular cause, activity or course of action, that is God revealing your calling to you. God is a God of abundance. This is evident in everything we see in nature. God gives us a multiplicity of gifts, talents and interests. Our personality and skills profile make us naturally suited to excel in certain roles. This makes us an asset to serve others and thereby glorify Him. If we listen to His voice and take note of our experiences, we will be able to spot the openings and opportunities He provides for us to deploy our gifts.

> *Calling is all-encompassing. It goes beyond spiritual roles. It includes both paid and unpaid work.*

Many people make the mistake of restricting 'calling' to 'spiritual roles'. Members of the clergy often speak of being called for ministry. It is true that some people are called to carry out spiritual roles, but calling goes beyond spirituality. We are called to serve in every conceivable role imaginable to serve human needs. If you have a passion for caring, God may call you to work in the health and social care sector. If you are good with numbers or computers, there are roles to play in accounting, science and engineering. Others are gifted and wired to serve in creative roles (writing, music, cooking, drawing, painting, design, etc.), practical roles (building, manufacturing, labouring, etc.), sport roles, speaking roles, and so on. The list is endless. There is at least one distinct role for every one of us.

In the same way our body has different parts with different functions designed to give us life and good health, God gives us different roles to fulfil His purpose on earth. Referring to roles in the church, for example, Paul puts it this way:

"We have different gifts, according to the grace given to each of us. If your gift is prophesying, then prophesy in accordance with your[a] faith; if it is serving, then serve; if it is teaching, then teach; if it is to encourage, then give encouragement; if it is giving, then give generously; if it is to lead, do it diligently; if it is to show mercy, do it cheerfully." Romans 12: 6–8

Every role is important in God's eyes, even though society assigns different value to them. Within the church, for example, vocational ministry roles are not superior to those roles devoted to cleaning and maintenance of the building. 'Ministry' is about serving and honouring God with your gifts and talents. No matter where you serve or what you do, you can serve and honour God. Roles within the church or secular roles are of equal importance to God when you are living out your calling. God would not call someone to be a builder if they were not creative, precise, practical and skilled with their hands. You must be gifted in the areas in which you think you are called and have a burning passion for the tasks involved.

Calling is not restricted to paid work. Neither is it restricted to serving in the church or ministerial calling. It is about service to others, no matter where or how this is performed. It includes service to our families, community or using our gifts to help the weak or bereaved. It should also be remembered that work is not restricted to paid work. God calls us to serve others through both paid and unpaid work. Paid work is not necessarily more important than unpaid work. The things we do outside of our paid work for our family and community may be the most vital aspect of our calling.

CONCLUDING REMARKS

God is real and takes an active interest in people's lives. He has a plan for everyone and has a variety of ways to call people to their divine assignment. God's plan for your life encompasses everything you do and even things you are not yet aware you are capable of doing. God is not just interested in what you do for a living. God is interested in your life as a *whole* and how you use your gifts and being to serve others, thereby bringing Him glory and fulfilling your purpose.

The call is for everyone – 'saints' and 'sinners' alike. It is not just for vicars and those in positions of leadership or authority. Whatever your image of God may be, remember God wants to talk to you and support you to carry out the various callings of your life. Don't see yourself as a product of accident or an afterthought. You are a precious part of God's plan and are lovingly created and equipped to play your part. Wherever you have a compelling and recurring passion, it is the voice of God guiding you towards your calling. Listen and respond to God's voice. And whatever you do, paid or unpaid, do it to the best of your ability and remember the ultimate purpose of doing it is to glorify your Creator.

END OF CHAPTER QUESTIONS

- What does God mean to you?
- How would you describe your relationship with God?
- How have your image and views about God changed over the years?
- Are you aware of your personal call from God?

Chapter Two

Made for a Calling

"There is no greater gift than to honour your life's calling. It's why you were born and how you become most truly alive."

Oprah Winfrey

In this chapter, I will discuss how you are shaped for your calling and the signs to alert you to your calling. For those who are trying to find their calling, I will also share with you a number of techniques that may be used to steer you towards your calling.

INTRODUCTION

Calling is about service and making the world a better place. Your calling is as unique as your fingerprints. Each person is uniquely created to carry out a God-ordained calling to meet the world's needs, even if we cannot always discern what we are called to do. Our calling may vary over time. God equips us with the skills, talents and personal qualities we need to fulfil our calling. God even sends the right circumstances, experiences and people in our lives at just the right time to help us to live out our calling.

Your calling encompasses your whole life. It is not about a single task. Nor is it merely what you do for a living. When you serve your family at home, you are providing a service to others and living out your calling. If you do volunteering work in your church or community, you are carrying out God's assignment. And when you use your gifts at work, you are also honouring your calling by making the world a better place for yourself and others. There is a universal call for us to work. Adam and Eve were put in the Garden of Eden to look after it. Work was built into God's creation.

MADE IN GOD'S IMAGE FOR A CALLING

Nothing exists in this world by chance. No one would create an object unless it serves a purpose. God has a reason for everything He created. As we look around us, we notice how plants, trees, animals and even the tiniest insects play a role in sustaining the life of others in the great circle of life. He gave human beings pride of place in His creation.

God did not mass-produce us. Each one of us was lovingly custom-made as unique masterpieces in His Image and Likeness. While this does not mean that we are God, made in 'God's image' suggests that each of us is endowed with God-like characteristics. We are not mediocre beings, designed to be subservient to others. We were all made equal in our Creator's image. Like God, we are 'creators'. When we compose a poem, write a book, design and construct a building, paint a landscape, invent a product, bake a cake or cook a meal, we are demonstrating what it means to be made in God's image. This ability to create places us above animals and everything else that God created.

We are distinct from the rest of creation by having a body, mind and spirit. We have a spirit modelled on God's own spirit. It is this spirit that gives each of us an in-built moral compass or conscience. Though not visible, our spiritual nature is as real as our physical characteristics. Each time we help someone, show empathy and compassion to someone, speak up against injustice or forgive someone for an offence, we confirm the moral aspect of what it means to be made in God's image.

God also made us for relationship and fellowship. This reflects God's Trinitarian nature – Father, Son and Spirit. He made man and woman for fellowship.

"The Lord said it is not good for the man to be alone."
Genesis 2:18

Every time we form a relationship or share with others, we are demonstrating the social side of what it means to be made in God's image.

God did not just make us in His Image. He had a plan for our lives which pre-dated our birth and even the creation of the universe. Earth was made to sustain us. He had a purpose for each one of us long before we were born.

"Before I formed you in the womb I knew you, before you were born I set you apart; I appointed you as a prophet to the nations." Jeremiah 1:5

He made us bespoke to fulfil His purpose. This includes every little detail about us; even the colour, length, mass and thickness of our hair.

"And even the very hairs of your head are all numbered." Matthew 10:30

No two persons are alike. No two persons share the same fingerprints or the same DNA. No two persons think alike or have the same experiences, relationships or attitudes. We perceive reality differently. Our bodies are shaped differently. Even the way we walk and talk is unique to us. God is a God of variety. Imagine a world with some seven billion people, all made in God's image yet unique and individual at the same time. Think too of the uniqueness of the zillions of people who were on earth before us and those who will replace us when we are no longer here. None of them were replicas or products of mass production.

God also gives us the gifts, talents, aptitudes, personality and experience that we would need to serve His purpose. No two persons have the same personality, aptitudes or abilities. This is because we are placed here to fulfil a different part of God's eternal plan. God created you for a purpose which only you can fulfil as part of your divine destiny. We are given everything we need to perform our particular role. None of us is an afterthought. Each of us is an integral part of the 'cosmic whole'. The world needs something which only you can provide. You alone have what it takes to meet that need – the vision, the passion, the drive, the skills and knowledge to create something to meet the world's need.

Self-acceptance

Before we can find our calling, we first need to embrace and celebrate our uniqueness. We need to rid ourselves of self-doubt and stand tall in our own space. This means owning our experiences, personal traits, culture, colour and everything that makes us unique and different from others. You need to be proud of your identity or the things that make you uniquely *you*. These include all your characteristics, including those others see as weaknesses. What the world sees as 'weaknesses' may be your greatest strengths.

The people who succeed and lead fulfilling lives are those who accept themselves as they are. Rather than trying to imitate other people's appearance or mode of operation, they celebrate their uniqueness and make it a habit of doing things their way. They are, in effect, a 'brand'. In the sphere of business, this is what accounts for the success of people like Richard Branson, Bill Gates, David Beckham, Sharon White, Iyanla Vanzant and Oprah Winfrey. In music, it is what made musicians such as Aretha Franklin, Rhianna, Bob Marley, Louis Armstrong, Pavarotti and Prince great. In science, it is what made Einstein stand out. In sports, it is what makes Jessica Ennis-Hill, Lewis Hamilton, Usain Bolt, Cristiano Ronaldo and Mohammed Ali legendary. Ali was well-known for his mantra *"I am the greatest"*. This does not mean that Ali was comparing himself to anyone. He knew the meaning of Victor Williamson's dictum, *"Being a one of a kind means we are automatically the best in the world at what we do"*.

When you accept yourself the way you are, it is easy to step into your calling. You become a trailblazer, not a conformist or plagiarist. By definition, creative people are original. They remain true to the image in which God created them. They do not measure themselves against society's standard or what the media disseminates as 'normal' or 'acceptable' in terms of body size, image or behaviour. They love themselves the way they are. They have confidence in themselves. Their self-esteem is healthy and they do not attach any significance to criticisms and praise from others.

Poor self-esteem can cause people to miss their calling. It can lead to fear of taking risks and moving out of our comfort zones. It can cause us to over-rely on other people's opinions to validate our actions and decisions. Poor self-worth can also cause us to abandon our calling the moment we encounter obstacles and setbacks. This is especially the case when we do not conform to the norms and values of the structures around us.

You need to be comfortable in your own skin and show up in the world. There are people who detest seeing themselves as they are in a mirror. Some even spend large sums on cosmetic surgery, tattoos and body piercings to enhance their appéarance or to gain acceptance from their peers.

How to recognise you are being called

Finding your calling is not always straightforward. It tends to evolve over the course of your life. It also involves navigating twists and turns, breaking down barriers, and decoding signs which are not always clear. Everyone gets inklings of what they are here to do. Here are some signs to alert you to your call:

Callings are patient and recurrent – One of the clearest signs you are called to do something is a recurring thought or idea that keeps seeping into your mind. The thought may leave you momentarily but, like the melody or words in a song, it will keep coming back to you. It will spring into your mind when you are engaged in your daily activities or when you are unwinding and taking a break. There is no set time for the thought to emerge. It may even leave you for long periods, but rest assured that it will recur. The thought will keep recurring and tugging at your heart until you have embraced it and made a conscious decision to act upon it. Invariably, the thought relates to a problem in your community or somewhere in the world which requires your particular blend of aptitudes and skills.

Synchronicities and divine alignment – Things will happen to steer you towards your calling or to confirm that your calling is real and not a passing whim. All of a sudden, people, events and circumstances will come together to make your calling possible. If your calling is to write a book on a certain subject, you may notice other books or materials pertaining to the topic of interest. The Universe will send people to help you with the things that you would otherwise struggle with. This may be help with funding, research, drafting or finding suitable publishers. The right doors will open for you at just the right time.

Feeling of peace – Initial feelings of anxiety or fear will give way to courage and an unshakable confidence that you will succeed in your call. You will feel as though you are being guided by a Higher Power. Everything associated with your calling will feel right. There is no longer a void. You now feel empowered, whole and complete. You know where you fit in this beautiful universe which God has provided for you to enjoy. You are comfortable in your own skin, and at ease with the changing fortunes of life. You have a quiet inner confidence that everything you need to fulfil your calling will fall into place even though you may not have all the answers or know-how.

Right experiences – You will have light bulb moments on how your experiences fit together and shape you for your calling. You will come to realise that none of your experiences over the course of your life are useless and redundant. You will see the pain from a broken relationship, a financial hardship, discriminatory treatment in the workplace, an accident or any other setbacks in your life as a stepping-stone to help you to do what you are called to do. It is as though these experiences have been preparing you to execute your true calling. Your journey to your calling will be every bit as exciting as the destination itself.

Ignition of passion – Your calling ignites your passion and brings you to life. It is what makes your heart sing. You will feel a surge of energy. You will feel that you are doing exactly what you were born to do rather than what others influence you to do. You will not only do it well, but you will be passionate about what you do. Your life will have meaning, and your energy level will be high as you do work which you deeply enjoy and care about. You will feel victorious and alive. Your work will feel effortless, exciting and fulfilling. It will not be seen as yet another boring task to be completed. The motivating force for your work will be service to others – whether local or worldwide – rather than money, power or status.

Pain and barriers – Although the universe will send people to help you to fulfil your calling, you should also expect opposition from detractors or 'call-blockers'. Some of the 'call-blockers' may be friends and even family members who may not welcome the change in your life. Some people may feel you are losing the plot or you do not have what it takes to realise your calling. Some may even feel threatened by your strong sense of purpose and your quest to give expression to your talents. You will find yourself wanting to change and improve things to make a greater contribution to society. Those who are wedded to the status quo will criticise you and may be tempted to sabotage your call. Rather than be discouraged by criticisms and dirty tricks, see this as further confirmation of your calling and use it as a motivating force.

Sense of divine guidance – You are able to see the opportunity in every situation life throws at you. You will understand how even seemingly adverse circumstances are sent to help you grow to fulfil your destiny. You become an optimist. You focus on your purpose, not the obstacles in your way. You are able to see the 'big picture' for your life. This allows you to spend your time and energy on work and activities that align with your calling. You now know what really matters – what battles to fight and what to let go. Divine guidance allows you to discern the difference between a 'skirmish' and a 'war'. People without a true calling easily wither and fall by the wayside when faced with adversities. Faith and guided support from God are essential to keeping us aligned to our calling.

Sense of self-worth – Your calling boosts your self-esteem. When you are on the right path, you have confidence in your abilities and recognise the value of your work and other activities. You now have a reason for getting out of bed and a reason for living. Job satisfaction and personal satisfaction now become the norm in your life. Your life falls into place. You attract success, good health, happiness and fulfilment. Your success becomes the natural by-product of living moment by moment, day by day in alignment with your purpose. You feel the need to accept each new day with gratitude.

In contrast, when you are disconnected from your calling, you will feel like you are sleepwalking through life. Sleepwalkers live a life of drudgery and tedious routine.

Their view of life is limited to what they see every day – going to work to get paid for work they do not enjoy, returning home, eating, watching TV, engaging in social media, sleeping and having fun in between with addictive behaviours. Sleepwalkers fear change. Although they are not happy with their life, they are afraid of taking action. They do not believe in themselves. They prefer to follow others rather than valuing their own gifts and talents. They waste a lot of time on complaining about life and making excuses for not taking steps to improve their life.

FINDING YOUR CALLING – DISCOVERY METHODS

> *"For the past 33 years, I have looked in the mirror every morning and asked myself: "If today were the last day of my life, would I want to do what I am about to do today?" And whenever the answer has been 'No' for too many days in a row, I know I need to change something."*   Steve Jobs

If you are not using your unique gifts and talents to do the things that you are passionate about, this is a sure sign that you are not living in alignment with your calling and life purpose. If your job drains your energy rather than energise and empower you, you are clearly out of sync with your calling.

To find your calling, start by finding out what lies 'within you', while seeking or creating opportunities for deploying your unique talents and qualities. There are as many roles to be performed in this universe as people. You should avoid societal pressures and any urge to follow the crowd. Just as you were made as an original masterpiece by your Creator, in the same way you need to resist any pressure or temptation to adopt another person's calling. If you do, at best you will be a second-rate performer. People who excel in their chosen vocations are the ones who tap into their natural, God-given talents day after day and chart their own unique path to heed their soul's calling.

Oprah reminds us, *"You have to find what sparks a light in you so that you in your own way can illuminate the world"*. Spiritual coaches tell us that every one of us is naturally endowed with an Internal Guidance System to direct us to our true calling in life. We feel joy, enthusiasm, and unlimited energy when we engage in an activity that resonates with our purpose. In contrast, anything that generates feelings of high levels of stress, depleting energy levels, struggle, and boredom is a sure sign that we are off course.

In his book, *Divine Alignment*, Squire Rushnell, uses the concept of a God Positioning System (GPS) to explain this idea of an in-built Internal Guidance System. A God Positioning System gives the same benefits as a Global Positioning System, but it is infinitely more intelligent and reliable. Rushnell explains this GPS as follows:

"Right from birth, we come equipped with a highly sophisticated navigational package that — through an internal voice of intuition and godwinks — divinely aligns us with people, as well as events, who assist us in reaching our destiny and keep us from losing our way." p1

Your GPS is your personal navigator with the power to guide all aspects of your life. If you talk to your Navigator through prayer or other means you can find your way to any destination and solve any problem. You can find the answer to the question — what is my personal calling? Simply ask, listen and act.

Back in 2005, personal development coach, Steve Pavlina, wrote a popular blog on *'How to discover your life purpose in about 20 minutes'*. Although he used the word 'purpose' in the title, he actually meant 'personal calling'. In his own words,

"I am not talking about your job, your daily responsibilities, or even your long-term goals. I mean the real reason why you are here at all — the very reason you exist."

https://www.stevepavlina.com/blog/2005/01/how-to-discover-your-life-purpose-in-about-20-minutes/

Pavlina made the insightful point that your inner self already knows the answer to why you were born and what you are here to accomplish. All you have to do is simply ask *"What is my true purpose in life?"* until you finally reach the answer that makes you cry.

The exercise is comprised of the following steps:

1. Set aside quality time (30 minutes is suggested) on your own in a quiet environment.
2. Make sure you have writing material to hand or some means for note-taking.
3. Take a few minutes to calm your mind by focusing on your breathing.
4. Write at the top of the page *"What is my true purpose in life?"* and provide the answers that come to mind.
5. Write all thoughts that come to mind, however random. For every thought that emerges, continue asking that same question – *"What is my true purpose in life?"*

Pavlina suggests it usually takes about 15–20 minutes to clear your head of all the clutter and preconceptions you might have about your purpose. He writes:

> *"The false answers will come from your mind and your memories. But when the true answer finally arrives, it will feel like it's coming to you from a different source entirely. For those who are very entrenched in low-awareness living, it will take a lot longer to get all the false answers out, possibly more than an hour. But if you persist, after 100 or 200 or maybe even 500 answers, you'll be struck by the answer that causes you to surge with emotion, the answer that breaks you."*
>
> http://www.stevepavlina.com/blog/2005/01/
> how-to-discover-your-life-purpose-in-about-
> 20-minutes/

As you go through the process, you may find yourself generating similar answers to the question. You may even find your thoughts going off on a tangent. In some cases, you may feel a surge of emotion, but not strong enough to cause you to cry. This indicates that you have identified an aspect of your purpose. You should highlight such answers and return to them to generate other clues. Keep on asking the question until you find the answer which causes you to break down in tears.

If this method does not appeal to you, there are many other approaches that can help you to find your calling. These involve asking a series of 'discovery questions' to uncover what makes your heart sing. In all cases, you will be guided by your soul's infinite wisdom. Your soul will answer in one or more of the many ways in which it communicates with us. This may be through changes in our emotions, feelings, energy level and sense of balance. It may also guide us through images, signs, moments of synchronicity and intuition. Your soul knows. As you carry out these exercises, watch out for the things that give you a surge of energy, positive emotion, passion, excitement, and joy. This is your inner guidance system confirming you are connecting with your calling.

I have grouped the call discovery methods under the following headings – 'pray and listen', 'wound of wisdom', 'passion', 'secret fantasy', 'humanitarian' and 'eulogy' techniques.

Pray and listen technique

"Ask and it will be given to you; seek and you will find; knock and the door will be opened to you."

Matthew 7:7

This is a variation on the approach proposed by Pavlina. This involves praying and asking God to reveal your gifts and calling. Find a quiet place where you can be alone with God and simply ask: *"Lord, what are my gifts and what am I called to do?"* The answer may come in many different forms, so keep an open mind and wait with expectation. It may be in the form of intuition, a hunch, telephone call from someone, dream, message or sign or object steering you towards an opportunity and other guidance. God will speak to your heart to take note of your calling when it comes.

For this approach to work, you need to have a relationship with God. You will never hear God's voice if you are not spiritually in tune with Him. Once you ask, you must trust Him to answer your prayer. You must also slow down so that you can hear the whispers of your soul and notice any signs from a Divine Source.

You need to demonstrate faith and patience. You need to listen attentively to hear God's call. It may take time for you to hear the call but once you find it you will know. You will feel a sense of relief, freedom and deep peace. You will find yourself taking steps towards your calling with a calm feeling that success is inevitable. Before long you will find yourself serving others in roles which tap into your gifts. This will feel natural and effortless. Your heart will be engaged in your work, not just your head.

THE WOUND OF WISDOM TECHNIQUE

This is about turning your wound into wisdom to serve others. If you have experienced and overcome a major adversity in your life — such as unemployment, debt, loss of a loved one, accident, illness, or other significant losses — turbulent events as these may serve as a launch pad for your calling. Who is better able to give advice about how to deal with losses than the person who has faced losses and overcome it? Purpose can be found through pain. Pain leads to growth. It acts as a wake-up call so that we can see more of our potential. C. S. Lewis writes:

> *"God whispers to us in our pleasures, speaks in our conscience, but shouts in our pains: it is His megaphone to rouse a deaf world".*
>
> (Lewis, C. S. *The Problem of Pain*, San Francisco: Harper, 2001)

> *Purpose can be found through pain. Pain leads to growth. It acts as a wake-up call so that we can see more of our potential.*

Consider this example of how pain and suffering can lead to purpose and calling. When Cindi Lamb and Candace Lightner lost their children in accidents caused by drunken drivers, they were inspired to form Mothers Against Drunk Driving (MADD) to raise awareness of the dangers of driving under the influence of alcohol and drugs. Today, MADD is saving lives, not just in the United States but globally. MADD operates over 600 chapters all over the United States, as well as having offices in Canada, Australia, New Zealand and England. These two resilient mothers turned their adversity into something positive, something which will make a difference to humanity long after they and their children are gone from this earth.

Perhaps you too might choose to use your adversity to make a positive contribution to the world. Start by asking yourself the following questions and see whether this ignites a spark within you to help others.

- What are the main challenges or adversities you have overcome so far in life?
- How did you overcome these challenges and difficulties?
- What did you learn about yourself in the process of overcoming them?
- How can you help others to turn their pain into a gain?

THE PASSION TECHNIQUE

Your passion can help you find your calling. Begin by looking at the type of activities you like to do. Think about all kinds of activities – those relating to work, home and your personal life in general. Remember, your calling embraces your whole life. It is not as narrow as your job or career.

They should be the activities that make you come to life; activities that energise you and are as effortless and natural to you as breathing.

Some questions to consider are:

- What do you consider to be your strengths?
- What unique gifts, talents and skills do you possess?
- What do you enjoy doing?
- What activities are you passionate about?
- How do you feel when you are doing such activities?
- What makes you feel really alive and energized?
- How would those close to you describe your strengths?
- If you had to teach something, what would it be?

STEPHEN WILTSHIRE'S PASSION FOR DRAWING

Stephen Wiltshire, British architectural artist, is a good example of someone who found their calling by simply doing what they enjoy doing. He was born mute and did not learn to speak until the age of nine. His first words were 'paper' and 'pencil'. He was diagnosed as autistic at the age of three. Known as the 'human camera', Wiltshire has the amazing gift of drawing city landscapes and other objects from memory after seeing them just once, usually from a brief helicopter ride. He is internationally renowned for his talent and has gained numerous awards, including Member of the Order of the British Empire for services to art.

THE SECRET FANTASY TECHNIQUE

People often hold secret fantasies of the things that are important and meaningful to them. Just as in their early childhood years, they make-believe and role-play their heroes. They tell stories about how they would like to spend their time, write film scripts on the screen of their mind and act out the stories.

Here are some questions that may steer you towards your calling:

- Who do you most admire?
- What qualities do you admire about these people?
- What would you do if you knew you could not fail?
- When you fantasize about your obituary, what would you like it to say?

Oprah Winfrey's childhood fantasy as a talk show hostess

Oprah Winfrey is a good example of someone who used the fantasy technique to find her calling. As a young child, Oprah Winfrey spent much of her playtime 'interviewing' imaginary characters. Born in humble circumstances, she played games interviewing her corncob doll and the crows on the fence of her family's property. Winfrey later acknowledged her grandmother's influence, saying "it was Hattie Mae who had encouraged her to speak in public and [gave her a positive sense of herself]" (cited in Mel Novit. "Oprah: Talk Show Dynamo Treats the Audience Like a Friend", *Syracuse Post-Standard*, September 14, 1986, p.A9). Today, Oprah is a multi-billionaire media proprietor, talk show host, actress, author, producer, and philanthropist.

The Humanitarian technique

Purpose can be found through responding to problems around you. Think about the things that need changing in your community and the wider world. Some of these may be social, economic, political, technological and environmental. You may have just what it takes to make a positive difference. Consider these questions:

- If you could change one thing in the world, what would it be?
- Have you got what it takes to help fix this problem?

How Kenneth Behring found his purpose

American billionaire entrepreneur and philanthropist, Kenneth Behring, found his calling late in life when he set up a number of charitable organisations. These included the Wheelchair Foundation in Blackhawk, California, to provide free wheelchairs for people with physical disabilities in developing nations. He also established the Global Health and Education Foundation to promote good health, leadership development, museum and education programmes.

For the first time, he began to experience feelings of joy, peace, happiness and a deep sense of fulfilment. Prior to his humanitarian work, he felt empty despite living in a mansion, owning a jet, yacht, vintage cars, and having a fortune of over 500 million dollars. (Extracts from his autobiography – *see* Behring, Kenneth, *The Road to Leadership: Finding a Life of Purpose*, Blackhawk Press; 2013).

The eulogy technique

This approach helps you to identify what is truly important to you and the impact you would like to have on the world. If this is not what you are currently doing, it will reveal what you need to change and may spur you to make changes in how you live your life.

Start by visualising the end of your life and funeral. As you lie on your death bed and review your life, consider the following questions:

- Who would you like to be present?
- What would you like to have achieved?
- What legacy would you like to leave to the world?
- What would matter the most at the end of your life?
- What would you like those present at your death bed and funeral to say about the way you lived your life?
- What would you like your headstone to say about you?

The answers to these questions may either validate or challenge the way you are currently spending your time and resources. It will help you to understand your priorities and inspire you to make changes. Be grateful that you are still alive and have the opportunity to live out your true calling. Now imagine that you only have three years left to live. How would you spend your life?

REFLECTIONS ON YOUR ANSWERS

As you consider these different approaches to uncovering your calling, spend some time reflecting on your answers. Notice how you are feeling about each answer. What do the answers have in common? Which group of answers give you a feeling of passion, motivation, excitement, balance and joy? Which ones make you feel emotional and tearful?

As stated before, we are all born with an Internal Guidance System to signal to us when we are acting in alignment with our true purpose. Remember that the things which give you passion, excitement, joy and cause you to feel emotional or tearful provide a clear indication of your purpose.

- What type of career or vocation seems to gel most with the things that excited, moved, and really energised you from this exercise?
- Is this the type of career or vocation you are currently engaged in?
- Have you identified any talents or qualities that you have not used much to date, and that you now feel the need to use to serve others?
- Are you now ready to step out of your 'comfort zone' and embrace your personal calling?

CONCLUDING REMARKS

Calling is about service to God, the people around us and the world as a whole. It encompasses all aspects of our being and doing. It is about using our unique combination of gifts, talents, aptitudes and experiences to respond to the world's needs. Listen to your heart and be guided by your passions. God is within and around you and will guide you towards your true calling. Don't let your head talk you out of your calling.

Embracing your personal calling is about taking concrete actions to live in alignment with your calling day by day. When we live in alignment with our calling, we feel joy, fulfilment and freedom. We flourish as we use our gifts and talents to help those around us. If your life feels like an uphill struggle and meaningless, it is a sure sign that you have missed your call. Keep listening to God and respond with obedience when you hear His voice. In later chapters, I will spend more time discussing how God communicates with us and how to hear His voice.

END OF CHAPTER QUESTIONS

- What is calling you?
- What do you feel passionate about?
- What steps will you take today to start living in alignment with your calling?

Chapter Three

Who God Calls:
Lessons From Biblical Call Stories

"Wherever God has put you, that is your vocation. It is not what we do but how much love we put into it."
Mother Teresa

The previous chapter considered the 'why' of calling. I argued that we are placed on earth to serve others and make our unique contribution to bring honour and glory to God. In this chapter, I will build on this premise by looking at the 'who' of calling. None of us is excluded from God's call. The call is universal. No one is excluded on grounds of their *'brokenness'*, gender, race, nationality, creed, age, sexual orientation, health, disability, material status or any other personal characteristics. The people called by God, and who respond to His call, are also carefully prepared for their divine assignments. All that God expects from them is their willingness to honour the call and follow their passions.

GOD'S CALL IS UNIVERSAL

God's call is not restricted to a privileged few. He is a God of justice and fairness. He gives every one of us a chance to contribute to the world and serve humanity with the unique and distinctive array of gifts and passions He lovingly places in us.

In schools, workplaces, churches and all walks of life, people have favourites. People get excluded from teams, opportunities and privileges for all kinds of reasons. Those in positions of leadership and authority may overlook people simply because they belong to a different social or ethnic background than themselves. It may be as subjective as not liking the colour of their hair or eyes. Perhaps they appear to have too many qualifications, too much confidence or presence, or are too independent in their thinking. Over the years, I have seen people excluded from teams and company benefits because of their sexual orientation, ethnicity, class background and even their accents. Wherever we live, newspaper headlines are often filled with complaints and allegations about racism, ageism, sexism and other types of discriminatory practices.

God is a God of equality and diversity. It is interesting to note that the Bible begins with a declaration that God made everyone equally in His own image and likeness. This included males and females.

> *"So God created mankind in his own image, in the image of God he created them; male and female he created them."* Genesis 1:27

Throughout the Bible and other sacred Books, we see how God has called people from all backgrounds, in spite of their 'brokenness', to serve His greater purpose. The Apostle Paul told the Corinthians:

> *"Brothers, think of what you were when you were called. Not many of you were wise by human standards; not many were influential; not many were of noble birth."*
> 1 Corinthians 1:26

Paul was making the point that you do not have to be a celebrity or someone of privileged background for God to call you to service. In the rest of this chapter, I will further the discussion and show how God has called ordinary people for His purpose, in spite of their age, gender, health and their past behaviour.

GOD CALLS YOUNG PEOPLE

You are never too young or too old for God to call you and use you for His purpose. One of the best known call stories in the Bible is God's calling of young Samuel.

Samuel was only 12 when God called him to be a prophet and a leader for Israel. Samuel did not recognise God's voice. He had not heard God's voice before. We are told that it was rare for God to speak audibly to anyone at that point in Israel's history. Visions were also rare. This was a time of corrupt practices in Israel and God withdrew from communicating with the people. In Eli's own household, his sons engaged in pagan and adulterous practices. They regularly slept with the servant women in tent meetings, worshipped idols, and corrupted the sacrificial system.

Samuel served faithfully in Eli's household and assisted in the service of the sanctuary at Shiloh where Eli was a priest. Unlike Eli's sons, Samuel was loyal to God and found favour with Him. It should be remembered that he was a miracle baby, born to Hannah who was unable to conceive. Hannah constantly prayed to God for a child and vowed she would dedicate him to God's service.

God called Samuel four times during this time. Not surprisingly, the young boy mistook God's voice for Eli's voice. The first three times he ran to Eli and woke him up. Eli later realised the call was from God and taught him how to respond. If the call comes again, he should say *"Speak, Lord, for your servant hears"*. Samuel did as he was told and God gave him his divine assignment.

The Lord said to him:

> *"Behold, I am about to do a thing in Israel at which the two ears of everyone who hears it will tingle. On that day I will fulfil against Eli all that I have spoken concerning his house, from beginning to end. And I declare to him that I am about to punish his house forever, for the iniquity that he knew, because his sons were blaspheming God, and he did not restrain them. Therefore I swear to the house of Eli that the iniquity of Eli's house shall not be atoned for by sacrifice or offering forever."*
>
> 1 Samuel 3 (11–14)

Eli had failed in his duties to restrain his sons from their corrupt practices and was equally culpable. God announced to Samuel that judgement would be carried out against Eli's household. His family line would now be wiped out. The priesthood which they had monopolised since the time of Moses and Aaron would be taken away and given to another.

A part of Samuel's divine assignment was to lead this change. Samuel grew in stature and the Lord was with him:

> *"All of Israel from Dan to Beersheba knew that Samuel had been established as a prophet of the Lord."*
>
> I Samuel 3:19–20

He became Israel's leader and God's representative throughout Israel. He encouraged the Israelites to return to the Lord and stop worshipping false gods.

In the course of Samuel's assignment, we also see God using him to fulfil the calling of another remarkable young man. God called David in his teenage years. When Israel was languishing under Saul's despotic rule, God directed Samuel to choose a replacement king from Jesse's household. David went on to rule Israel for 40 years.

God called David even though he was not Jesse's strongest, brightest or best looking son. God's guidance to Samuel was to ignore the sons' outward appearance and look instead on their heart. Young David, the afterthought, was the only one of Jesse's sons to meet God's requirements. Yet David was not perfect. He was a womanizer and a murderer. He committed adultery with Bathsheba, Uriah's wife. He refused to take responsibility for her pregnancy, and devised a plan to kill Uriah when his cover up of Bathsheba's pregnancy failed.

GOD CALLS WOMEN

God's divine plan includes women from all backgrounds. Some were widows, virgins, orphans, married, prostitutes and of different ethnic groups. There are 188 women explicitly named in the Bible. I will focus mainly on the life of Deborah and Esther to discuss how women were used to achieve God's purpose. I will also examine the lessons from their call experience.

DEBORAH AND ESTHER

God used Deborah as a prophetess, judge, military strategist and leader at a time when Israel had no kings. For 20 years, the Israelites had been oppressed by Jabin, the King of Canaan. With the help of the military commander, Barak, she waged a battle against the forces of King Jabin and Sisera and defeated the Canaanite armies. Under her leadership, Israel enjoyed 40 years of peace.

Deborah was the only female judge in Biblical times but was not the only woman who was called by God to be a prophetess. There are many others and their successes speak volumes. Some of the more notable female prophets include Huldah, Miriam and Noadiah. Huldah is best known for confirming the authenticity of the Torah, which is the bedrock of Jewish Scripture. The then king, Josiah, called on her wisdom to interpret this lost Book of the Law instead of her male counterparts like the prophets Jeremiah, Zephaniah and Habakkuk.

God can use an orphan woman, labelled as a concubine to achieve great feats. Esther was a Jewish orphan living in exile in Persia. She was brought up by her older cousin, Mordecai, and became a member of the harem of the Persian King Xerxes. Her Jewish background was hidden from the King. She later became queen to the King when the reigning Queen Vashti was deposed for not obeying her husband's orders. Mordecai found out about a plot to kill the King and shared the news with Esther, who duly informed the King. The King ordered the assassination of the two plotters and appointed Haman as second-in-command over the kingdom.

Haman insisted that all the King's subjects should bow before him as a mark of deference to his position in the royal court. Mordecai refused to obey this command. When Haman found out that Mordecai was Jewish, he designed a plot to have all Jews in the Persian kingdom killed and confiscate their property. He used his influence in the court to secure the king's consent to this massacre. Of course, the king did not know that Queen Esther was also a Jew.

Mordecai found out about the edict to wipe out all Jews and encouraged Esther to use her influence with the King to save her people. Although she was the Queen, she was not allowed to see the King unless invited by him. Going before him without an invitation could end her life. The King had not had any contact with her for 30 days. Esther realised she was called by God to save her people. Mordecai bolstered this belief and spoke about God's purposeful timing:

> *"For if you remain silent at this time, relief and deliverance for the Jews will arise from another place, but you and your father's family will perish. And who knows but that you have come to the royal palace for such a time as this."* Esther 4:14

She stayed obedient to her call and came up with a plan to gain the King's attention. She invited the King and Haman to her house for a meal and informed him of Haman's evil plot to destroy her people. She won the King's favour and he ordered the assassination of Haman on the same gallows which Haman had built for Mordecai's execution. The King issued a decree authorising the Jews to defend themselves. Mordecai was rewarded by the King for his loyalty and was promoted to the post of second-in-command, which was previously held by Haman. It was he who had found out about an earlier plot devised by two of the King's courtiers to have him killed. For her part, Esther received Haman's estate and grew in influence.

Although God is not mentioned anywhere in the book of Esther, God's hand was clearly at work in the events that unfolded in Esther's fortunes. God put her where she needed to be at the right time to free the Jewish people. Today, the Feast of Purim is still celebrated to commemorate the rescue of the Jews by Esther. She risked her life to save them from genocide. By honouring her call, Esther rose from an orphan and a concubine to become Queen of Persia. With King Xerxes, she had a son, Darius II, who later went on to rebuild the holy Temple in Jerusalem. Mordecai, for his part, became King Xerxes' deputy. They were ordinary people like us. They became great because they used their God-given gifts and were obedient to God's call. Esther's gifts were her beauty, charm and courage. Her true calling was to save the Jewish people, not to gratify King Xerxes' pleasures.

OTHER CALL JOURNEYS INVOLVING WOMEN

Like Deborah, Miriam was identified by the prophet Micah as one of the three leaders God chose to lead Israel out of Egypt:

> "I brought you up out of Egypt and redeemed you from the land of slavery. I sent Moses to lead you, also Aaron and Miriam."
> Micah 6:4

Throughout the Old and New Testaments, women from all backgrounds have been called by God to play crucial roles, even when they would normally be excluded in today's society. Consider the following cases.

Sarah was in her 90s when she gave birth to Isaac and the bloodline of Abraham. Elizabeth, Rachel and Hannah also experienced long seasons of infertility before they were called. God's purpose and plans include prostitutes, people labelled as social outcasts and single women. Rahab was a prostitute. Ruth was a gentile and widow. Naomi was a widow. Hosea's wife was also a prostitute.

Jesus' disciples or followers included women, some of whom had ill health and other disabilities. Mary Magdalene, His principal female follower, was said to possess seven demons. Today, this would be defined as mental illness. Tabitha, also known as Dorcas by her Greek name, was also one of Jesus' disciples (*see* Acts 9:36). She became ill and died during her call. She was brought back to life by St Peter. The Samaritan woman at the well was a harlot.

Mary Magdalene is undoubtedly the most popular woman in the Bible. In the New Testament, her name is mentioned more often than some of the 12 Apostles called by Jesus. She was present with Jesus during His crucifixion, burial and resurrection. Significantly, she was the first to see Him after the Resurrection. Not only did she see Him, but she was commanded to share the good news with the disciples.

After Simon, Peter and the disciples examined Jesus' empty tomb, they left, but Mary Magdalene stayed outside weeping. We are told in the Book of John:

> *"Jesus said to her, "Mary". She turned toward him and cried out in Aramaic, "Rabboni!" (which means 'Teacher'). Jesus said, "Do not hold on to me, for I have not yet ascended to the Father. Go instead to my brothers and tell them, 'I am ascending to my Father and your Father, to my God and your God'." Mary Magdalene went to the disciples with the news: "I have seen the Lord!" And she told them that he had said these things to her."* John 20: 16–18

The way Jesus treated women provides a striking contrast to how they are viewed nowadays in society. He was happy to have women using their gifts to help Him carry out His own purpose. He commissioned Mary Magdalene to be the very first Evangelist. He could have given this role to Peter or John or one of his other male disciples but, instead, He chose to use Mary for this purpose. Although the Gospel of Mary was excluded from the Bible, this book presents Mary Magdalene as a leader of Jesus' disciples. She witnessed to the disciples after Jesus' resurrection and inspired them to spread Jesus' message throughout the world.

Contrary to what some people think, the Apostle Paul also provided opportunities for women to exercise their call in leadership and other roles. In Philippians 4:2, he refers to Euodia and Syntyche as his fellow evangelists. In Romans 16:1, Phoebe is described as a minister of the church at Cenchrea. In Romans 16:7, Paul refers to Junia as an outstanding apostle. In Romans 16:3, he refers to Priscilla as another of his co-workers. These examples of women in teaching and leadership roles are at odds with the often quoted passage by Paul:

> *"A woman should learn in quietness and full submission. I do not permit a woman to teach or to assume authority over a man; she must be quiet."*
>
> 1 Timothy 2:11–12

Nowadays, we see gender inequality in all areas of society. As in Biblical times, our societies remain patriarchal. Men continue to wield power and shape the rules of engagement between themselves and women. In spite of sex discrimination legislation in many countries, women's roles are primarily seen as child-bearing, caring, and house-keeping. Although women are now a growing part of the labour force, leadership roles continue to prove elusive. Men are more content to see women in caring, personal assistants, administration and support roles.

Rather than challenging gender discrimination, society's views of women are reinforced by the church. The Roman Catholic Church and The Orthodox Church exclude women from becoming priests. The Church of England spent almost 100 years resisting the ordination of women to the priesthood. The question of women's ordination to the priesthood was formally considered in 1920 at the Lambeth Conference, the worldwide gathering of Anglican bishops, but was greeted with resistance. Further discussions of the issue in subsequent years received a similar fate. It was not until 1992 that the General Synod voted to permit women to be ordained as priests. The first women priests were ordained in 1994 and it was not until 2014 that the General Synod finally agreed to open up all orders of ministry to both men and women. Rev Libby Lane made history when she became the first female UK bishop in January 2015.

Although society was organised on patriarchal lines in Biblical times, women were still able to honour their calls.

St Paul declared:

> *"There is neither Jew nor Gentile, neither slave nor free, nor is there male and female, for you are all one in Christ Jesus."* Galatians 3:28

God promised everyone that *"In the last days, [He] will pour out [His] Spirit on all people.* **Your sons and daughters will prophesy***, your young men will see visions, your old men will dream dreams."* (Acts 2:17, emphasis added) This promise gives the lie to those who hold onto the backward notion that a woman's place is in the home and that those who teach and have positions of authority in the church and elsewhere in society should be men.

GOD CALLS MENTALLY ILL PEOPLE

The state of your physical or mental health does not preclude you from God's call. In today's world, people with mental health problems are often stigmatised and overlooked by employers and those in positions of power. They are one of the groups less likely to secure suitable employment, gain access to government resources, and to be accepted in mainstream society. Yet, in God's eyes, we are all the same. He accepts us as we are and use what we have to serve His purpose. Let us consider the case of Elijah.

Elijah, the prophet, is the classic Bible example of someone called by God to serve His purpose in spite of his mental health problems. In the course of performing his calling, he fell into an acute depression and became suicidal. The state of his mental health is clearly evident in the words he uttered in the wilderness following a confrontation with Queen Jezebel's false prophets and threats on his life. He asked God to take his life:

> *"I have had enough, Lord," he said. "Take my life; I am no better than my ancestors."*   1 Kings 19:4

Elijah's name reflects his calling – his name means *"My God is Yahweh"*. He was called by God to urge the people of Ancient Israel to stop worshipping false gods and return to the true God. After the reign of King David, Israel was ruled by a succession of evil and idolatrous kings. The most infamous of these kings was King Ahab. It is said that:

> *"Ahab ... did more to arouse the anger of the Lord, the God of Israel, than did all the kings of Israel before him."*   1 Kings 16:33

The people worshipped the Canaanite gods Baal and Ashtoreh. Baal was the favourite deity of Jezebel, King Ahab's wife. To please his wife, Ahab had altars erected to Baal and Jezebel ordered the murder of God's prophets.

Elijah's own life was under threat, but he remained obedient to God's call. In spite of God's warnings to the people to return to true worship, they continued to worship false gods. God decided to punish them with a severe drought.

He chose Elijah to announce His curse to King Ahab:

> *"As the LORD, the God of Israel, lives, whom I serve,*
> *there will be neither dew nor rain in the next few years*
> *except at my word."*   1 Kings 17:1

This miracle was performed through His faithful servant Elijah. He prayed for God to withhold rain from Israel for three-and-a-half years so that the people would know the true God. His prayer was answered. The drought brought about a severe famine throughout the whole of Israel.

The prophets of Baal were humiliated when they were rendered powerless to end the drought and the suffering it had brought about. In a showdown at Mount Carmel with 450 prophets of Baal and 400 prophets of Asherah, Elijah tested the power of Baal against the Jewish God's power. He challenged the people to choose the true God:

> *"Elijah went before the people and said, 'How long*
> *will you waver between two opinions? If the Lord is*
> *God, follow him; but if Baal is God, follow him.'"*
>   1 Kings 18:21

Two altars were erected, one for the false god Baal and the other for the Jewish God. Wood was placed on the altars. Two oxen were slaughtered, cut into pieces and laid on the wood. Baal's prophets were then invited by Elijah to pray for fire to light the sacrifice. The false prophets called on their god to send down fire. They prayed from morning until nightfall, but to no avail. Elijah mocked their efforts:

> *"Shout louder!" he said. "Surely he is a god! Perhaps he is deep in thought, or busy, or traveling. Maybe he is sleeping and must be awakened."*   1 Kings 18:27

They responded by slashing their skin and pouring the blood onto the sacrifice, but nothing happened.

It was now Elijah's turn to prove his God's power. To make the task more difficult, he drenched the altar of his god with water from four large jars. Then he asked God to accept the sacrifice and to send fire from heaven. Fire fell from the sky and consumed the offering, altar, water, and even the dust around it. Elijah then ordered the deaths of the prophets of Baal.

The people fell on their faces in awe, shouting,

> *"The Lord, he is God; the Lord, he is God."*
> 1 Kings 18:39

Elijah ordered the people to slay the 850 false prophets. Elijah's prayer was answered. After this, he further demonstrated God's power by praying for another miracle. He prayed for God to restore rain on the land and the rain came immediately and ended the famine.

Elijah devoted his entire life to restoring true worship in Israel and to exhorting the people to worship the true God faithfully and with their whole hearts. Through his miracles, he exposed the deception of Baal's false prophets and demonstrated that Israel's God was the only true God.

In spite of his mental health problems and personal weaknesses, God was able to use Elijah for great things. It is said that people like Hagar, Moses, Naomi, Hannah, Saul, David, Solomon, Nehemiah, Job, Jeremiah, John the Baptist and Judas Iscariot all suffered with mental health problems. God does not discriminate against people with mental health problems.

GOD CALLS CRIMINALS AND WRONGDOERS

Both in the Old Testament and New Testament we also find evidence of how God called criminals and wrongdoers to perform his works. Moses was a murderer. Before he became an Apostle, Paul was a mass murderer. David had one of his best men in the army killed so he could steal his wife.

Let us look closer at the first two cases and draw out the lessons about how God calls people and prepares them for their call.

Moses was called by God to lead the Hebrew people (the children of Israel) out of Egypt where they were abused and used as slaves. God gave him his mission by appearing to him in a burning bush.

When the pharaoh of Egypt passed a decree for all new-born Hebrew boy babies to be drowned at birth, his mother hid him. The Pharaoh resorted to this measure to limit the growth of the Hebrew population in Egypt. After three months, she placed him in a wicker basket and placed it in the Nile River reeds. The baby was rescued and adopted by one of the pharaoh's daughters. By a miraculous act, he was soon reunited with his mother when the Pharaoh's daughter employed her as a 'maid' to help her care for the baby.

He enjoyed the privileges of a prince in the Pharaoh's household. When he grew up he visited his own people. He became incensed when he saw one of the Pharaoh's overseers ill-treating a Hebrew. He killed the Egyptian overseer and the pharaoh ordered his execution. He fled to Midian to save his life and later married Jethro's daughter. It was there he received his call from God in a burning bush to return to Egypt to lead his people out of bondage and bring them to Canaan. It took 40 years for him to free his people. It was during this period he received the Ten Commandments from God at Mount Sinai and presided over some amazing miracles, including the parting of the Red Sea and the drowning of Pharaoh's forces when they refused to free God's people. It was left to his successor, Joshua, to complete the work he began. He reached as far as Mount Abarim where he could see Canaan. He died at the age of 120 after the Hebrews entered the promised land.

Moses' call may be compared and contrasted with Paul's call. Before his call, he was known as Saul. Newspapers' headlines are often covered in news about the persecution of Christians in places dominated by other religions. Open Doors (UK), a Christian missionary organisation, estimates 100 million Christians face persecution, particularly in countries such as Pakistan and Saudi Arabia. The persecution of Christians is nothing new. In Jesus' time, this was the fate of the early Christian Churches.

One of the worst perpetrators of this crime was Paul. By his own admission, he was responsible for the deaths of many early Christians.

> *"I persecuted the followers of this Way to their death, arresting both men and women and throwing them into prison."* Acts 22:4

He devoted his life to stop the growth of Christianity. He was party to Stephen's murder. Saul watched the cloaks of those who stoned Stephen to death. After Stephen's killing, Saul went from house to house to round-up Christians for punishment and imprisonment.

It was while he was on the road from Jerusalem to Damascus to arrest Christians that the resurrected Jesus appeared to him in a great light. He was struck blind for three days.

> *"Meanwhile, Saul was still breathing out murderous threats against the Lord's disciples. He went to the high priest and asked him for letters to the synagogues in Damascus, so that if he found any there who belonged to the Way, whether men or women, he might take them as prisoners to Jerusalem. As he neared Damascus on his journey, suddenly a light from heaven flashed around him. He fell to the ground and heard a voice say to him, 'Saul, Saul, why do you persecute me?"* Acts 9: 1–4

His sight was restored by Ananias of Damascus. Saul received a new call. He relinquished wrongdoing and began to preach that Jesus of Nazareth is the Jewish Messiah and the Son of God. The transformation was profound. He became Paul, the Apostle, one of the greatest evangelists of his day in spreading Christianity throughout the Roman world. His writings account for most of the New Testament of the Bible. Like the early Christians, he experienced suffering and persecution in spreading the Gospel. His former friends now sought to kill him.

"Yet Saul grew more and more powerful and baffled the Jews living in Damascus by proving that Jesus is the Messiah. After many days had gone by, there was a conspiracy among the Jews to kill him."

Acts 9:22–23

The stories of these wrongdoers prove God can use even criminals and those written off by society for great deeds. Anyone can turn their lives around, no matter how heinous their crimes or how many years they have spent in prison.

God knows that even criminals have skills and experiences which He can use as part of His divine plan. We have seen how Paul transformed from using his zeal and energy to persecute Christians to using those same qualities to preach Christ's teachings all over the Roman world. We also have a large number of modern day examples of ex-convicts who have been rehabilitated and are now using their skills to serve society in endeavours aimed at reducing crime and creating safer societies.

A notable example is Frank William Abagnale, whose criminal past inspired the blockbuster film *'Catch Me If You Can'*. By the age of 21, he was a genius in fraud and the art of conning all kinds of people. He committed numerous crimes, masquerading as medical doctor, airline pilot, lawyer and college professor. He was released early from prison on condition that he used his expertise to help the US government combat fraud. He now runs a highly successful fraud consultancy business serving corporations and law enforcement bodies all over the world.

Jesus' interaction with the thief crucified next to Him on the cross shows that criminals can be called and redeemed from their misdemeanours at any stage in their life. There is hope for everyone. So long as we are still alive, God can use us to accomplish His mission on earth, no matter what mistakes we have made or what offence we deliberately committed. God knows that none of us is perfect.

Some of the most successful people in the world today were once ex-convicts. They include icons such as Malcolm X and the rappers 50 cents and Jay Z (*see* http://www.arrestrecords. com/15-surprising-ex-convicts-who-made-it-big/). There is hope for everyone. God does not write off any of us, no matter what our past is. There is a clear lesson here for decision-makers, policy-makers and opinion-formers in our society in how to treat people.

> *"If my people, who are called by my name, will humble themselves and pray and seek my face and turn from their wicked ways, then I will hear from heaven, and I will forgive their sin and will heal their land."*　　2 Chronicles 7:14

LESSONS FROM THESE CALL STORIES

These case studies reveal a number of lessons about calling. These lessons should help to clarify some of the misunderstandings surrounding calling.

First, *God uses ordinary people to accomplish his purpose.* His criteria for selecting people to serve Him are different from ours. You don't have to be a celebrity or someone from a privileged class to be called. Your background, physical characteristics, personal traits, mistakes or past do not exclude you from His call. He is happy to use the weak and marginalised as much as the strong and privileged to serve His purpose. Adulterers, murderers, prostitutes, physically and mentally ill people, inarticulate and stuttering people like Moses and Jeremiah, and orphans like Esther can all achieve extraordinary deeds for His glory if given the opportunity and supported during the execution of their calls. God knows that none of us is perfect. With Him, there is no discrimination. It does not matter who we are or who we used to be. God calls all of us to serve His greater purpose.

> *What the world sees as our weaknesses, God sees as our strengths. He takes us as He finds us and uses what we have to achieve His greater purpose.*

Second, *calling is about service to others in a variety of roles*. It is more than paid work or working in a vocational capacity or being called to the priesthood. God expects us to perform the services we are gifted to do and to do them with love and a sense of duty. We live out our calling when we use our gifts, experiences and resources to serve others. We can serve Him by using our gifts to meet people's everyday needs. Consider the following examples. Hannah served God by praying and giving birth to Samuel well beyond child-bearing years. She used her gifts of faith, patience and her mothering skills to bring up young Samuel to be a loyal servant to God. Esther used her gifts of beauty, charm and courage to save the Jewish people from genocide. Ruth obeyed her calling and served God by comforting and supporting Naomi, her grieving mother-in-law after she had lost her husband and two sons. She then accompanied Naomi to Israel and worked hard to support both herself and Naomi. Ruth tells Naomi:

> *"Don't urge me to leave you or to turn back from you. Where you go I will go, and where you stay I will stay. Your people will be my people and your God my God."*　　　　　　　　　　　　Ruth 1:16

> *Living out our calling is more than doing paid work, vocational and pastoral duties. It includes the services we provide to our families, church, community, and the wider world. We honour and glorify God when we serve others and show love, empathy and a sense of justice.*

Third, *God calls people in different ways.* He uses the means that they are likely to understand. Sometimes, He also uses the means that will get their attention. Some of those who He call need 'wake-up calls' or 'Damascus moments', like what happened to Saul. In Samuel's case, he called his name twice – *"Samuel! Samuel"* in the middle of the night. He also called Moses by name. Moses saw a bush on fire, then a voice called *"Moses! Moses"* out from the flames. God used a messenger to deliver Esther's call. Her cousin, Mordecai, convinced her that she was being called by God. He used Samuel to choose David. He used a catastrophic sign to call the Apostle Paul. Paul found himself engulfed in a bright light which left him blind for several days, followed by a voice *"Saul, Saul, why are you persecuting Me?"*

Fourth, *those called by God are expected to respond with obedience,* even if they feel they are not fully equipped to do what God wants them to do. Obedience to God demonstrates our faith that He will guide us through our call. Elijah had unwavering faith in God in the face of mounting opposition and threat to his life. He carried out God's instructions with obedience and dealt a heavy blow against false gods in Israel.

Fifth, *when you are called you will face trials and challenges.* We should pursue our call even if it means challenging the status quo and defying those in authority. Elijah was willing to confront the false prophets of Baal and rid Israel of idolatry. His showdown with the prophets of Baal on Mount Carmel was a necessary part of his assignment. He invited the nation to choose between the Lord and Baal. Through this famous showdown, he proved beyond doubt that Israel's God was the only true God. Jezebel was irate at the loss of her prophets and sought to have him killed. In a similar manner, Esther was willing to challenge the status quo. Esther went to see the King without being summoned by him, even though this was against the rules. The penalty for doing so was death, but this was the only way to get the King's attention. Mordecai also challenged authority. He refused to bow before Haman as this would elevate him above the King and God. Both Esther and Mordecai did what they thought was right, even if it meant losing their lives.

> *"Whenever God calls us to a task, He will equip us."*
> Michael Youssef

Sixth, *God provides for us when we accept our call.* He remains with us throughout our call experience; and He will send the right people, resources and circumstances into our life at the right time to support us. For example, when He called Moses, He said,

"I will be with you. And this will be the sign that to you that it is I who have sent you: when you have brought the people out of Egypt, you will worship God on this mountain."   Exodus 3:12

God never goes back on His promises. In Moses' case, He showed His presence by performing a number of miracles through Moses. When God instructed Moses to throw down his staff in front of Pharaoh, it became a serpent. When Pharaoh refused to set God's people free, He sent a plague of locusts on Pharaoh and the Egyptian people. He empowered Moses to use his hand to turn the sea into dry land so that the Israelites could cross the water, then allowed the water to return and drown Pharaoh and his entire army (*see* Exodus 14: 26–28).

We also saw how God provided for Elijah during his call. He was outnumbered 450 to one but that did not stop him from taking on Baal's prophets. When his life was threatened by Jezebel, he fled to the brook Cherith. God took care of his needs. Ravens brought him food. When the brook became dry, God sent him to live with a widow. The widow only had a small amount of oil and flour but God multiplied it so that there was enough to meet their needs. God also comforted and strengthened him during his depression. An angel was sent to provide for his physical and emotional needs (*see* 1 Kings 19: 5–8).

Seventh, *we should wait patiently while God prepares us for our call.* It is human nature to want instant answers to their prayers. God always hears our prayers and chooses to answer when the time is right. Hannah had to wait until when the time was right for God to answer her prayer. She remained barren for years and was ridiculed by her rival Peninnah who had children for the husband which they both shared. Hannah wept bitterly and prayed until God finally answered her prayer. She conceived and gave birth to Samuel. Esther had to wait for the right time before she could save the Jewish people. Moses had to spend 40 years in the desert looking after sheep before he was called to deliver the Israelites. When God delayed their journey from Egypt to the Promised Land, the Israelites complained:

> *"They travelled from Mount Hor along the route to the Red Sea, Or the Sea of Reeds to go around Edom. But the people grew impatient on the way; they spoke against God and against Moses, and said, 'Why have you brought us up out of Egypt to die in the wilderness? There is no bread! There is no water! And we detest this miserable food!"*   Numbers 21:4–5

God's timing is perfect – never early or never late. We often feel frustrated while we are waiting for God to answer our prayers. We should see the period of waiting as preparation time. God takes time to prepare us for our call. He calls us when we are equipped and ready to take up our assignment. God will ensure that everything falls into place when the time is right. We should trust Him. Even when it seems that nothing is happening, the invisible hand of God is always at work for our greater good. Esther's call made this abundantly clear. God is not mentioned once in the ten chapters that comprise this Book. Yet all the events reported in this Book were shaped by God's intervention.

CONCLUDING REMARKS

God's purpose and plans include everyone. No one is excluded on grounds of age, gender, race, class, faith, sexual orientation, health status, nationality, disability, physical characteristics, material or personal circumstances, past mistakes or any other grounds. God is a God of justice and fairness. He gives every one of us a chance to contribute to the world and serve humanity with the unique and distinctive array of gifts and passions He lovingly places in us.

God knows none of us is perfect. He even uses our 'brokenness' as part of our gifts to serve others. God's way of doing things is different from ours. We live in a world where all forms of discrimination are present in our dealings with each other. We choose people for roles simply because they share our characteristics, values or beliefs. Rather than helping them to heed their call, we sometimes act as 'call-blockers'.

God made every one of us unique in His image and likeness and wires us to carry out our divine assignment. He expects us to use our gifts to serve others and make the world a better place, even if this means challenging the status quo. Every one of us has something valuable to contribute and He expects us to heed our call. This will be further developed in the next chapter where we will examine some more 'call stories' – secular callings – to complement the Biblical case studies reviewed in this chapter.

 END OF CHAPTER QUESTIONS

- Do you think God calls everyone to serve His purpose on earth?
- How has He called you to serve others?
- How has He equipped and prepared you for your call?
- What, if anything, is stopping you from living out your call?

Chapter Four

Who God Calls:
Lessons From Modern Call Stories

God continues to call people to do His work in the world. In this chapter, I shall discuss six contemporary call stories (including my own call journey) to complement the Biblical stories discussed in the previous chapter. Again, I will draw out the lessons from these call experiences.

INTRODUCTION

The case studies selected for this chapter are diverse and varied. They include my own call story and the call experiences of a 30-year-old scientist (Dr Garrick Wilson), a transsexual woman and former teacher who converted to the Catholic Church and is a strong advocate for LGBT rights in the Church and in schools (Dr Claire Jenkins), a Church of England vicar (Reverend Sonia Barron), an 85-year-old retired care-giver and nurse (Mrs Deloris Hall) and a musician and leader of a dynamic choir (Freddie Kofi, founder of Present Future Generation Choice).

The call journeys of these remarkable people reinforce the lessons from the Biblical call stories. They show how God equips ordinary people to do extraordinary deeds when they stay obedient to their call. They also show that we cannot run away from our call, notwithstanding our tendency to remain within our comfort zone and play safe.

DIANNE SEALY-SKERRITT'S CALL – SOCIAL JUSTICE CHAMPION

God has called me to be a pioneer and champion of justice and fairness for all. This passion for fairness and justice has underlined everything I have done in life from childhood to the present. As a young child, I was driven to ensure everyone was treated fairly and had access to good things. I can recall sharing personal possessions such as new clothes and money willingly with other children. The feeling of satisfaction which I receive from helping other people is indescribable. Joy, energy and vitality surge through me and every cell of my body feels super-charged with positive emotions.

In my various professional roles, my sole focus has always been to do my part to create a world where people are treated equally and with respect, regardless of their physical or socio-economic characteristics. My mission was justice for all and I learned that issues of justice arise in every sphere of human activity and social relationships.

Long before I became a Social Worker in Nottinghamshire County Council and an Equality and Diversity Officer in the Church of England, I was able to see and respond to people's different needs with fairness and justice. Later in my travel agency business, for example, I did not just process orders for flights from customers as other travel agents do. I was driven to respond to all aspects of my customers' needs and go the extra mile for them. Unlike other travel services, people could call at any hour of the day or night to book flights, especially when they had to travel to the Caribbean or other parts of the world at short notice in response to the loss of a loved one or other emergencies. Customers did not just come to book flights. They often brought their problems with them and I found it natural to help them find solutions. I provided a welcoming environment. This included complimentary hot and cold beverages. For those with medical needs, I would organise appointments and assist with ordering prescriptions in time for their departure.

In my Church of England role, I have seen how God intervened to help me to secure justice for asylum-seekers against the odds. My job in supporting delivery of The Rainbow Project involved promoting racial equality and cultural diversity, as well as providing practical and spiritual help for people seeking sanctuary – more commonly known as asylum in the United Kingdom. I served in this role for almost ten years until I retired at the age of 70. While I have enjoyed all the roles which I have assumed over the course of my working life, this job was probably my most fulfilling. Some of my achievements in the role were sheer miracles. God clearly wanted me in that area of work.

I have fought many battles for asylum-seekers to be treated as real people with rights and needs that must be respected. All too often their claims were dismissed as bogus without the authorities even trying to gather and investigate the facts about the cases. I worked courageously to challenge stereotypical attitudes and to correct misconceptions about people seeking sanctuary. For those who had genuine reasons for seeking asylum, I helped many to secure the right to remain in the UK where they are now making a positive contribution to our society.

One of my most notable achievements concerned a woman from the Congo who had entered the UK on a false Belgian passport, a crime for which she was held in a detention centre without bail. She couldn't speak any English so I went to visit her with a translator. After seeing her I couldn't sleep. The woman was in her 40s but she appeared to be in her late 70s. She was genuinely fleeing from war and persecution in the Congo, a war which had already claimed the life of her husband. In my view, she had already suffered enough and should not have to suffer further indignity. No one was willing to bail her. When I made representation to my employer on her behalf, their response was *"We don't put up bail for people, we're a project"*. I challenged them to do something on this occasion, even though they had never done anything like this before, and in spite of the risk that the woman could abscond.

At this point, they agreed that we could put the surety up, so long as we could find a domestic address to bail her to as a business address would not be accepted by the court.

Not to be deterred, I spoke to some people from the local Congolese community and found a suitable bail address. When the case was heard, the court granted the woman asylum and she is now making a positive contribution to UK society. The woman has been transformed economically, physically, emotionally, psychologically and spiritually. She is unrecognisable. The woman I first met was so distraught and full of despair that she appeared to be almost twice her chronological age. Her transformation was wonderful to see. Moments like these fill me with joy. This is the joy that comes from staying obedient to our call. It is impossible to put a monetary value to this feeling.

God will never tell us to do anything we are not able to accomplish. Even if the task is new or seems to be impossible, always be prepared to follow God's voice. I can remember taking on another difficult challenge whilst I was delivering The Rainbow Project. The task seemed impossible. The family was from Pakistan and all hope of being granted asylum seemed lost. They were being detained in Yarl's Wood and deportation was imminent. I kept thinking that there must be one more thing we could do. I suggested prayer. We held a vigil one evening and people from all faiths and nationalities took part. It was a great show of unity and love to see so many people coming together at short notice to support the cause of this family. Clearly, they were responding to God's message.

The demonstration of solidarity led to a review of their case. The family was subsequently granted asylum and is now settled in the United Kingdom. We were left in no doubt that God's Hands were at work in this case. I acted on what God told me to do. I simply listened to Him and obeyed. Throughout the whole proceedings, I felt an inner calm. Something told me that what we were doing was the right thing and, notwithstanding the hurdles, everything was going to work out fine.

I can only ever remember losing one case, involving a woman from Malawi. I prayed relentlessly with her whilst she was held in detention and asked God to grant her asylum in the UK or some other suitable country. After going through the appeal process, she was eventually deported to her country. A couple of years later she became married to a citizen of the United States where she is now happily living and working. God clearly had a better plan for her.

This is how the lady describes the situation:

"Although I was deported after several detentions I believed that God had not forsaken me. I was still following Him and praying until God himself opened another massive door for me. God will always perform His word for sure and His plans are not our plans and they are of good, not evil. I believe God had made me go through all the challenges I faced. He knew me. He knew His purpose for me. He knew what He had called me to do and He knows what's in my future. He has placed me where I am at this very moment for a reason and I trust He is working everything out."

Although our calling often comes with challenges and responsibilities, there are also huge rewards. There is no greater feeling of personal fulfilment than knowing you are doing God's work and helping others. Through my calling, I have encountered people whom I would not otherwise have met and been to places that I could only dream of. For example, my calling has taken me overseas on numerous occasions to countries such as Austria, Budapest, Burundi, Egypt, Spain, The Holy Land, Zambia and Zimbabwe.

A calling is never complete until we die. My calling continues to unfold. Writing this book is a part of it. Who knows where this will lead me? God has already revealed to me that I am called to start a community project in Burundi. At the time of writing this book, I am planning this project in parallel. Although I do not have all the answers to the many challenges posed by the Burundi project, I am fully confident that God would never plant this seed into my heart without creating the conditions for it to germinate and flourish to meet the needs of the Burundi people. I will remain faithful to my heart and simply follow my passions for as long as I am here. There is nothing more fulfilling than when you honour your call and use the talents that God has given you to serve others and make the world a better place.

DR GARRICK WILSON'S CALL – SCIENTIST AND LIFE COACH
This is the call journey of a very extraordinary young man from the African-Caribbean community. A key message from his call experience is that it does not matter where or how

you start your journey. What matters is how you respond to the events in your life and where you end up.

Dr Garrick Wilson is an emerging research scientist with expertise in the fields of liver pathology and vascular disease. He is the author of numerous publications in learned, high impact journals such as *Proceedings In the National Academy of Science, Nature Biotechnology* and *The Journal of Hepatology*. His work has identified promising treatment options for liver and cardiovascular diseases, which opened numerous opportunities for him to speak at national and international conferences attended by leading academics, clinicians and representatives from the pharmaceutical industry. He has collaborated or worked with world leading scientists who are known for their work on viral infection, liver inflammation, vascular disease and cancer biology. Notably, he has received several awards for medical research and mentors several Master and Doctorate degree candidates in the area of biological sciences.

He has been called to serve humanity in a variety of ways. At this phase in his life, the main focus of his call is personal development coaching. It is a call to help people to become the best version of themselves. He works tirelessly in pursuit of this goal by:

- connecting individuals to their purpose;
- providing them with access to networking opportunities;
- helping them to access top higher education institutions (including Oxbridge);

- providing personal development coaching (including effective communication and self-branding); and
- mentoring inner-city young people to stay off the streets, stay in school and grow up to realise their full potential.

Garrick is in no doubt that God has called him to do this work. When I asked him about the basis of this conviction, he replied as follows:

> *"I am reminded of the expectant turtle that leaves the deep blue sea and slowly journeys across the sandy beach to lay her eggs. She then covers the eggs under the sand and makes her way back to the sea. After a period of time, the eggs hatch and mother is no longer present to guide her babies. However, they immediately make their way towards the sea without any external instruction. I believe a similar principle applies to the call. We are deeply attracted to our calling. We are drawn to certain news reports more than others. We are affected by certain injustices than we are by others. Our attention is fine-tuned such that we are not 'doing' the call. Instead, we 'become' the call. It is therefore a lifestyle and this is the greatest indicator that we were born for this."*

The things that he does come naturally to him – it is life by design. He is in his element when he engages in these types of activities. He enjoys the transformation he helps to bring about in the lives of people from disadvantaged groups, many of whom would otherwise end up with unfulfilled dreams or as a burden to society.

Garrick knew from an early age what God was calling him to do. He told me that it was present in seed form from the outset. As he puts it:

> *"Whatever I am doing now or whatever I will strive to do later in life have already been done in seed form in my formative years. For example, in order to promote the educational aspirations of others, I had to first walk this journey. In the face of many odds, including being told that I was not good enough to study Science at university I persisted. Having experienced hardships and being from a single parent home, my hard work and discipline meant that I was able to study at a Russell Group University, work for one of the top ten universities in the world, and made presentations at leading institutions, including Oxford University. These experiences are among the first that have convinced me that I am called to pave a path for others who aspire to achieve."*

As with the other call stories which I have discussed in the preceding chapter, Garrick's journey confirms that a call experience is never a smooth process. It comes with challenges and crises. Like Joseph's 'pit experience' or Job's trials, Garrick had to deal with the challenge of growing up without the emotional, financial and practical support of his father. He had to deal with discrimination and stereotypical attitudes from teachers and authoritative figures who tried to block his call.

God led him through all these challenges and helped him to live out his calling. He remained obedient to God and allowed himself to be led. From early childhood, he realised that his relationship with God is important. He knew he could always pray to God and ask for help. Time and time again, God made Himself real in his life. He learned from a very early age that God sometimes answer prayers by changing him to be the solution to his own problem. He knew that he wanted to address large audiences one day and would smile at the thought of being a great orator and communicator. However, the very thought would leave him shaking with fits of nerves. His late grandmother, Advira Pennant, was a committed Christian and would remind him that prayer is the key to unlocking potential.

He soon noticed that the more he prayed the more that he was challenged to ask for opportunities to participate in weekly church services. Developing the confidence to stand up and speak to an auditorium of brilliant minds is no easy feat. The church has been a wonderful training ground for him; simple tasks such as reading the scripture during Sunday morning services nurtured enormous confidence. Moreover, he was frequently asked to be the speaker at the church's youth events, which helped to carve out his own unique brand of stage presence.

Garrick does not believe one can consciously plan a call or work their way to it by their own volition. In his own words:

> *"I believe God made every individual with a predetermined function for which they were born to accomplish. Every step taken in life leads one to this unique discovery providing that they are guided by the instinct to achieve and make decisions or take steps which are necessary to walk worthy of the call."*

Although Garrick has had to deal with 'call-blockers' along his journey, he was quick to acknowledge the role of those who served as 'call enablers'. He is overwhelmed with gratitude for their support:

> *"I have met some tremendously wonderful individuals along the way, including the author of this book, who – for reasons unknown to me – saw the best in me and supported me. They have helped me financially, practically and morally. Furthermore, being from a single parent home and seeing first-hand the sacrifices that my mother made for her children, this compelled me to pursue success. I believe individuals and experiences are the bedrock of defining moments that are integral to the call."*

What he may have lacked from not having a loving and supportive father in his life, his mother more than made up for it. Throughout his life, she has been his rock and has been unwavering in her support to him. In Garrick's words, his mother – Claire Pennant – *"stands in a league of her own; none can compare to the world's greatest mom"*. He is also grateful for the contribution of his aunts Rose and Concie Pennant, both teachers, who helped with homework, school supplies and cooked meals. His grandmother's support was invaluable; she was his spiritual and moral mentor. As a child, she taught him that *"the student who succeeds goes far above and beyond the required standard"*.

When I asked Garrick about whether he experienced any barriers to hearing and responding to God's call, he expressed the view that social and economic factors were potential barriers but somehow he managed to overcome them. It is easy to give up on your dreams and stay within your comfort zone when you are faced with financial challenges or conditions which are far from ideal. He could easily have followed his peers and abandoned his own call. Many of his peers chose the 'familiar' options for black boys; including pursuing a career in music or sport after leaving school. He considered this path to be *"perfectly aspirational as long as they were not just following the crowd or the normalized trend"*.

He was accused by them of 'selling out' and was often made to feel like a misfit because he no longer conformed to their perspective on life. They accused him of speaking like the white man and pursing a university course that was unfamiliar to individuals from his culture. Many of them failed to reach the glittering heights of musical or sporting success and they found a job, often low paid, in their local area. Soon after that, they started a family and some even ended up on the wrong side of the law. To Garrick's credit, he defied the odds and found a way of going to a top university to pursue his passion.

Our peers can also be a barrier to our call. Peer pressure needs to be managed carefully. Garrick pointed out:

> *"Long-standing friendships broke down because others failed to understand or support my calling. Every call is unique and it can often feel like a lonely journey which in itself can be a barrier because it will conflictingly position you to choose between salvaging relationships, taking on-board the contrary advice of others or being steadfast. You can waste a lot of time trying to hold-on instead of letting go."*

Garrick is now reaping the benefits of heeding his call. As he puts it:

> *"Responding to the call is to live on purpose; life doesn't feel like a chore or a mere career choice. One is awakened daily with a sense of vitality and a reason for being, this is beneficial for happiness and productivity."*

This contrasts with the lack of fulfilment experienced by those who burn themselves out day after day, doing jobs that make little or no use of their talents and aptitudes.

He has learnt a number of important lessons about how

God calls people. He reminds us that calling is, first and foremost, about service to others. It is an ongoing journey, not a destination. And you never know what you will encounter on the journey. As he puts it:

> *"The idea is always clearer than the how. You will not always know how it will get done. However, you should pursue the idea irrespectively because the pieces will always fit in place. The call is a journey – choose wisely who comes on your journey. Always remember that the call is never selfish – it is for service."*

For the person who is wondering, how can I serve others with my call? Garrick says *"serve from the area that you are gifted in"*. One practical example from Garrick is how he chooses to spend a portion of his free time reading, editing and advising on degree dissertations for university students from his community. He also helps to draft personal statements and CVs and arranges mock interviews as practice for the real thing. He recalls a conversation with a college biology lecturer who told him:

> *"Idea and reality do not live on the same street. Some privileged few succeed in this field because they had the opportunity to shape their idea through real experience."*

The lecturer was concerned that although he had potential he lacked the real experience of the privileged few.

He has since worked very hard to amalgamate his idea and his reality. In doing so he has now positioned himself to open opportunities that he never had for others by taking on young people interested in his field, to work alongside him throughout the summer holidays so that they can move their idea and reality into closer proximity. He advised *"use what you know best to shape at least one life positively; don't overthink it"*.

DR CLAIRE JENKINS' CALL – CHAMPION FOR LGBT RIGHTS

Dr Jenkins is a 67-year-old transsexual woman and a convert to the Catholic Church. She was married with four children until she transitioned from male to female at 50 years of age. In 2013 she was awarded a PhD from the University of Sheffield for her research into the effect of transitioning on the family members of transsexual people.

Dr Jenkins summarises her call as *"to improve the pastoral care of lesbians, gays, bisexuals and transvestites (LGBT) Catholics in the Church and in schools"*. She lives her call with passion and is making a big contribution to the lives of LGBT people. She promoted transgender equality in the trade union movement as vice chair of the National Union of Teachers LGBT advisory group for nearly 20 years. Dr Jenkins also has 22 years' secondary school teaching experience, 12 of which were as the deputy head teacher in a socially disadvantaged Midlands ex-mining town. Although she enjoyed her teaching role, she was forced to leave in order to transition.

Dr Jenkins is in no doubt that she is using her unique gifts, aptitudes, personality and experiences to do the work which God has shaped her to do. She found her call by using *Ignatian Discernment* principles and listening to God's voice for guidance.

IGNATIAN DISCERNMENT METHOD

Ignatian Discernment (based on the work of Saint Ignatius of Loyola, who founded the religious order called the Society of Jesus or Jesuits).

If you are not familiar with the Ignatian Discernment Framework for learning about your calling, here is the link to a very helpful introduction to this method – http://www.ignatianspirituality.com/making-good-decisions/an-approach-to-good-choices/an-ignatian-framework-for-making-a-decision

Ignatian spirituality is based on the belief that God is active, personal and accessible to everyone. The exercises are designed to answer the question: What more does God want of me?

Dr Jenkins was directed to the current phase of her call by joining and working with QUEST. QUEST's purpose is to provide pastoral support and proclaim the gospel of Jesus Christ in order to sustain and increase Christian belief among homosexual men and women. Through regular meetings with local bishops and other Catholic leaders, QUEST promotes LGBT inclusion in the life of the Catholic Church (for more details about QUEST, *see* http://questgaycatholic. org.uk/about/).

Her life experiences played a major part in her call. In *Straddling the Scalpel of Identity, My Earliest Memory*, Dr Jenkins writes candidly about how her sexual identity was established for her by her family through the simple act of filling out mandatory bureaucratic paperwork. She was registered as a male but this did not coincide with her lived reality. In her adult years, she has had to fight many legal and social battles to gain recognition for her true identity. In 1999 Dr Jenkins was still married to his wife and was the father of four adult children. When he changed sex and gender he became estranged from his family and had to contend with rejection and discrimination from individuals and organisations alike.

The inertia of the Catholic Church to accept LGBT initially proved to be a major barrier to hearing and responding to her call. Through various initiatives spearheaded by QUEST and its members, steps are increasingly being taken towards welcoming LGBT Catholics, parents and families into the Church's mainstream. However, in Dr Jenkins' opinion, the pace of change remains *"exceedingly slow"*.

When I asked Dr Jenkins about the benefits of following her call, she provided a clear and concise response: *"Happiness and delight – a feeling of rightness"*.

Looking at the attitude of the Church of England towards the LGBT community, it is clear that homophobic views are not just entrenched in the Catholic Church. The dominant view in the Church of England remains that *"homosexual practice is incompatible with Scripture"* (Lambeth Conference, 1998, Resolution 1.10). In 2007, the Anglican Church of Nigeria refers to homosexuality as *"a perversion of human dignity"*.

Not everyone within the Anglican Church shares such extreme views. Archbishop Desmond Tutu has been an outspoken advocate of LGBT rights and same-sex marriage. He described the oppression of gay people as the 'new Apartheid' and is on record as saying he would rather go to hell than worship a 'homophobic God'. His daughter, Reverend Mpho Tutu, had to give up her Anglican church license when she married her lesbian partner, Marceline Van Furth in December 2015. The South African Anglican Church is one of the many such churches that does not recognise same-sex marriage.

Churches should be inclusive organisations where everyone is welcomed, valued and treated with love, dignity and respect. Those who preside over our churches should help people to live out their calls. They should not be call-blockers. In the eyes of God, we are all equal. Regardless of our sexual orientation or our other characteristics, He has made us equally in His image and likeness. I will develop this theme further in Chapter Six which deals with barriers to hearing and responding to God's call.

REVEREND SONIA BARRON'S CALL – VICAR

Sonia knew her calling from a very young age. From the age of 15, she told me she felt called *"to share the good news of Jesus, initially to work overseas but it was not until I was 27 years old that I responded to this call to work as a missionary – teaching a variety of subjects in Uganda"*. Her ministry in Uganda heightened her spiritual awareness and closeness to God in a way that left her questioning what more God wanted of her. However, in the same way that she was resistant to God's call to overseas mission, she was unwilling to take the next step in exploring God's further plan for her life.

Her specific call to ordained, priestly ministry came in 2004 when minority ethnic Anglicans were invited to Bishopthorpe Palace by the outgoing Archbishop. The invitation was to explore how minority ethnic groups could participate more fully in the life of the church and be present at all levels of church life. She told me:

> *"I specifically remember walking to the chapel and the thought coming to my mind that the only way I could make a difference would be to be on the 'inside' and as I questioned what that would mean in practice the thought of ordained ministry came to mind."*

Since her prior experience of women in ministry had been negative, Sonia was initially reluctant to heed the call to ministry. However, as the impulse was so recurrent and strong, she decided to take action by consulting with her vicar. He was not a great supporter of the ordination of women and discouraged her from taking any further action. She did nothing further for a whole year. This later changed through a chance conversation with someone in the selection team at Church House, Westminster, who encouraged her to speak to the Diocesan Director of Ordinands (DDO).

But even this process wasn't straightforward. She recounted her experience:

> *"Because of my age the DDO decided to put me through as an Associate priest – a term which I didn't understand until I went to my Bishops Advisory Panel (BAP) and was asked 'How do you see your ministry working out alongside full time employment?' and I explained that I expected to be in full time ministry. However, after the BAP, I was sent to a Candidates panel and recommended for training for stipendiary ministry."*

It is not sufficient to hear God's call. We need to respond with obedience and faith. We also need to overcome our fear, pride and personal agendas and accept God's plan for our lives. Sonia almost missed her call because of *"my own personal desires and aspirations initially and as the process continued those who I would refer to as 'gatekeepers' such as my incumbent and the DDO."*

Her ministry is now making a positive difference to many people's lives. In Sonia's own words:

"I believe my pastoral ministry, in particular through the occasional offices, has made those to whom I minister view church in a different way. It has given them a sense of God being close to them, rather than it just being an event. The follow-up I do from these has meant that a connection with the church has been maintained and they know we are there for them every step of the way."

When I asked her about the main lesson which others can learn from her call, she replied without hesitation as follows:

"I think the most important lesson for me has been to trust that the way God leads is the right way even when obstacles or barriers are put in the way. It was important for me to meet someone who believed I was called and encouraged me to pursue this with my DDO – had it not been for him I don't think I would be in ministry today and it would have been a loss to the church and my life would not be as enriched as it is now knowing I am walking in God's way. I would encourage anyone who believes they are called to serve God in some way to find someone who believes in their call and can walk the journey with them until God's Will is done in their lives."

This is so true. It reminds me of young Samuel's call. Many of us need an Eli or a mentor to help us to discern God's voice and to pluck up the courage and obedience to carry out God's plan for our life. In the course of our call, we will encounter people who try to block our call. However, God will also send people to help us to find and fulfil our call. We need to allow ourselves to be guided by God.

MRS DELORIS HALL'S CALL – RETIRED NURSE AND CARE-GIVER

Deloris Hall is a retired nurse and care-giver. Aged 85, she is the mother of nine children and 30 foster children who she regards as her 'own children'. Although most of these foster children are now parents themselves, they have all chosen to remain as a part of her family and still call her mum. As I spoke to her about her call, I could not help noticing the array of cards, flowers and other gifts which she receives almost daily from those whom she has cared for over the years. A Mothers' Day card from Shereen, one of her foster daughters now aged 35, reads *"Happy Mother's Day. You will always be one in a million."*

As I listened to her account of her call, I was left in no doubt that everyone who had crossed her path would readily share Shereen's assessment. Helping and caring for people in need is what comes naturally to Deloris. She has devoted her whole life to this passion. She knew she was called to serve people in this way from an early age. As a child growing up in Jamaica, she was accustomed to seeing people poverty-stricken and struggling daily for survival. She told me about one of her early acts of kindness which required bravery and defiance of her parents. When she was 12, her parents briefly left her at home on her own. She saw this as the perfect opportunity to pack a bag of groceries from her parents' cupboards to give to her neighbours who lacked food. As she was hurrying to take the food to her neighbours, she fell and sliced her leg on a sheet of zinc. She picked herself up and carried on with the errand. Although her grateful neighbours did not notice she was bleeding, it was quickly noticed by her parents when they returned. Her parents reprimanded her, but this did not stop her from helping her neighbours in whatever ways she could.

At the age of 22, she emigrated to the UK on the *Santa Maria* ship to improve her economic fortunes so that she would be better equipped to help others. She was quick to point out she came on a luxurious ship, not a 'banana boat' as is often portrayed by the media. Her first job was to work in Chilwell Artillery where she made parts for guns. In those days (the 1960s), maternity leave and family-friendly policies were non-existent in most workplaces. She decided to leave this job when her employer demanded that she return to work days after giving birth to her baby daughter. She was subsequently employed by Raleigh Bikes before leaving to train as a nurse to do what she felt called to do – caring for people. She worked for Cedars Hospital in Nottingham for a number of years in care of the elderly. She fondly recalls her time caring for sick people in the terminal stage of their life and helping them to die comfortably and pain-free. She also worked for Social Services as a care-giver for elderly people, before leaving at age 50 to become a full-time foster parent.

She recounted many instances when her husband would return home to find strangers taking up sanctuary in their home. He would ask *"Who are these people?"* and she would simply reply *"They are God's people"*. This summarises how Deloris sees people: *"We are all one people, made by the same God in His own image and likeness. We are here to love and care for each other."* She exemplified that we do not have to be wealthy to be generous. We can start by sharing our time, our love and by showing empathy to others.

She told me how she decided to become a foster-parent when she learned about the pain and suffering of a restless five year-old girl who changed fostering homes as many as 15 times. She made contact with Social Services and offered to care for the child. She enquired about the child's family history and learned that she had two brothers aged four and seven who were being fostered in separate homes. She agreed to foster the child on condition that she became foster-parent for all three children. She felt instinctively that the girl's unease was due to her separation from her brothers. She was right. All three children lived with her until they became adults. Indeed, the girl ended up living with her until she was 35 years old. She is now a proud mother and a successful professional making a positive difference to other people's lives.

Deloris shared a number of mystical experiences about her call. She made the point that God calls us to follow Him in obedience before He calls us to do any form of work, whether paid or unpaid. There was a time when she did not know how to pray. During this period, she prayed a simple three-word prayer *"Lord, have mercy."* She repeated the same prayer day by day. One day, she found herself praying effortlessly and heard a voice encouraging her to start attending church. She obeyed reluctantly. When she went to church, the pastor asked if there was anyone visiting for the first time. She put her hand up and said *"I didn't want to be here but God sent me here"*. The congregation was moved by her simple testimony.

Since then, she has learned to recognise God's voice and God has guided her more and more to care for others. She recounted a dream where she was instructed by God to deliver a message to a family whose son had just carried out a major crime. Although she did not like to visit other people's homes, she managed to find out where the family was living and delivered the message. They were surprised she knew about their son's crime and was glad to receive the message. Although the message did not stop the son's punishment, it had the effect of restoring a loving and trusting relationship between the young man and his parents. Prior to her visit, his mother had decided not to attend the court hearing. However, Deloris reminded her that she was told in her dream that her presence in court would be a great blessing to her son. She later confessed to the joy and relief she felt when her son smiled at her behind the docks.

She spoke about some of the setbacks which she experienced during her call. On one occasion, she was gravely ill and required a major surgery. At first, she felt afraid. She found herself worrying about all the things that could go wrong with the operation and wondered about the wellbeing of her children and foster-children if she was no longer around to look after them. She prayed to God about her feelings and concerns. She listened and waited expectantly for an answer. She noticed a dramatic change in the weather. It was a dull and overcast day without a ray of sunlight. All of a sudden, the sun started to shine brightly and she felt a feeling of peace and relief. The fear disappeared and she felt a surge of energy. She packed her hospital bag and found herself looking forward to a stronger and healthier version of herself after the operation. The operation was a success. She was in no doubt that God had guided her through it.

When I asked her about the benefits of following her call, her eyes lit up and there was a long pause. Then she remarked, *"The benefits are too many – it would take years to tell you"*. I waited for her to tell me more without any further prompts. Rather than telling me more, she began to pray spontaneously and celebrate her blessings. In her prayer, I noted she thanked God for the gifts of a long life, good health, a wonderful family and her lovely home.

Her choice of adjectives to describe her home was apt in a certain sense. She could justifiably have used 'magnificent'. From humble beginnings, she is the blessed owner of a very large and spacious bungalow in a much sought-after part of South Nottingham. She earned £5 per week in her first job at Chilwell Artilleries and lived with her mum until she was able to live independently. Now living in her own home, surrounded on all sides by beautiful gardens and fruit trees, she told me she often hears from God whilst sitting outdoors among her plants. She referred to her garden as *"the garden of Eden"*.

In response to my closing question about what lessons others can learn from her about God's call, she replied:

> *"It is good to listen to the Lord. It is good to know Him and have a relationship with Him. You feel like a new person when you walk with God and do the work He calls you to do. I wish I had accepted Him earlier. I wasted a lot of time because of pride and ignorance."*

This is a lesson which is worth heeding. We cannot hear God's voice unless we listen. And if we cannot hear God's voice, we will miss our call and the tasks He wants us to carry out whilst we are here on earth. Deloris' call experience also reminds us that pride and ignorance can serve as barriers to hearing God's call. In Chapter Six, I will look at the question of barriers to hearing God's call and offer some guidance on how to become better listeners.

Freddie Kofi's call – musician and songwriter

Freddie describes his call as *"to communicate God's mission and commitment to social justice to the wider community through songs, creativity and advocacy. Secondly, it is to promote discipleship and service – especially towards songwriters, worship leaders and artists."* From an early age, he had a burning passion to sing, write and compose his own music.

This was what made him come to life and gave him a sense of fulfilment, meaning and grace. Freddie was in no doubt that God had put him on earth to serve Him through music and singing. And he responded to his call with obedience and faith.

People flourish when they follow their passion. This is clearly evident in Freddie's case. He is now a highly experienced and successful singer and songwriter with over 25 years of experience in the music industry. He is also the founder of the award-winning Present Future Generation Choir. Freddie has won many highly prestigious international awards in the music industry, including the British Academy of Songwriters' Best Song award for his original song 'Kiss'. Another of his songs, 'All of The Love', came second in the Rhythm and Blues category at the John Lennon Song Contest in New York. Freddie and his students have performed before many illustrious audiences. In 2010, Freddie and his students performed in Westminster Abbey for the Queen to celebrate Commonwealth Day. In March 2016, he was invited to the Prince's Trust's 40th Celebration at the London Palladium, where he performed a selection of original songs in recognition of his contribution to the music industry.

People and events played a significant role in moving Freddie towards his calling. His remarkable talents are admired by many. His musical performances are inspiring and have yielded encores and even standing ovations. This admiration for his talent from the public reinforces what Freddie already knew about his call. God often speaks to him through daily events such as those which make the news headlines. Many of his songs are a commentary on practical issues facing people in their daily living. His mission is to be God's ambassador in the world and bring about positive change through his music.

Freddie's view on calling and how God speaks to us is insightful and worth reproducing in full. In his own words:

> *"One of the foremost misconceptions about being 'called' by God, is that your calling will be confirmed by a particular voice from above or a dream or by some kind of mandate being bestowed upon you by another. Well, it can consist of all of these. But there is another element that was more akin to my own experience; it came through a variety of people who would hear my songs; they would then come up to me after performances or having heard my song on the radio and say things that resonated with me in my soul about the song. Yet it would still leave me speechless that a song I have written has had such an impact. One such song was, 'Too Quiet Too Long' – taken from my Journey: Destination Paradise album (2000 Littlegiant/Word/BMG) – which I wrote in the aftermath of the senseless, racially motivated murder of young, black Londoner, the late Stephen Lawrence. This song was woven into the fabric of my creative soul in a strange way. I recall feeling a real sense of helplessness about the whole situation and how the news reader would talk about the murder and then with a slight pause, go*

straight to the next news item which was about a dog almost drowning in a river or some other miscellaneous news summary. I remember thinking, 'No way!' I was astonished that whilst the news reader had an obligation to deliver 'all' news, it really hit me that this precious young soul has been reduced to a headline and that in spite of the horrific nature of this crime, the world still goes on; people still need to go to work and pay rent and make dinner and walk the dog. It may appear cynical or disrespectful, but it hit me so hard that it is a harsh reality regardless of how I or anyone else feels about the crime emotionally. It hit me right there and then in my living room that I knew I had been called and gifted as a songwriter and artist to shine a light on people's plight and help bring about change. So when the song was first performed live at Nottingham Playhouse in 2000, some seven years later, it drew a standing ovation from people who had never heard the song. I knew it right there and then that all my convictions made sense. I had never had that type of response to any of my songs before nor since. It was a pivotal moment. A real moment at the end of a long process I feel God used to confirm what I was called to do. This happened through people, events, circumstances and experiences."

He has been tested during the course of his call and still continues to face challenges. However, his deep belief in God and faith has convinced him that God would not give him an assignment without the means to accomplish it. Without this conviction, he could easily have stayed within his comfort zone and abandon his call. He started life as a school teacher but he knew this was not his real call and quickly gave up the classroom for the microphone. Rather than emulating other artists, he followed his heart and developed his own distinctive genre of music. Staying faithful to his call and following God's guidance is far more important to Freddie than pleasing the public and those who control the music business. He has had to learn to cope with those who doubted his vision and talent. He told me *"people will not always see what you see"*. His music is an integral part of who he is and the service he is here to offer to others. As he puts it:

> *"It's true to say that the pressure today is to do an album that fits onto a particular part of the shelf. There is also a great risk that you are going to do a great album that is not going to shift a unit, but I think there is a balance of saying what you like to say instead of saying what the people want to hear. This is where faith comes into it. I once used an analogy of a vision being likened to a pregnant woman where you know the baby will eventually come out but the only way you can stop it from happening is if you abort what God has put in you. I think those styles that I have incorporated in [my music] are true to my upbringing and as true to where God wants me today."*

Those who follow their calling often experience personal satisfaction and fulfilment. In Freddie's case, this takes the form of a deep sense of peace:

> *"Peace. Without doubt, peace. By peace, I do not mean you will be floating on air and enjoying a view from the mountains. What I mean is peace in the sense of knowing you are undertaking something with confidence that you are born for this. This means that even when things aren't going well, it does not cause you to throw in the towel, but inspire you to re-evaluate how you are trying to bring about your calling."*

Freddie also shares an important lesson which other people can learn from his call journey. It is important that they display the qualities of patience, persistence and self-belief. They need to allow God to guide them on *"when to wait and when to push through"*. They also need to have a strong self-belief and be resilient against criticisms. If he had listened to the criticisms from his detractors, he would either have missed his call or struggle through it. Freddie states:

> *"I have encountered many situations and people who have made it their personal mission to criticise me with the sole purpose of just making a negative point and scoring a point, with no solution on offer as to how and why I should either change or stop what I am doing."*

On the other hand, he acknowledges that other people can help us to live out our call. Freddie says:

> *"Good, honest friends are so pivotal and invaluable to carrying out your calling and Mission in this life. I implore any person who is a leader, to make it their priority to appoint a great assistant who does not covet your position, but whose focus is on ensuring you accomplish what God has asked you to do more effectively. This is what I feel is the first priority that underpins the effectiveness in the method and process of carrying out your calling."*

CONCLUDING REMARKS

These real case studies show men and women using their different gifts and talents in different ways to do God's work in the world. They show people doing work that is meaningful to themselves and others, rather than merely working to get paid at the end of the month or working for career advancement. There is a bigger purpose to what they do. They are not driven to do what they do in order to acquire money, fame, status or any of the other ways in which society defines success.

All six cases exemplify that when people accept their call, they stay focused on what God wants them to do rather than allowing themselves to be distracted by what other people want them to do. They seek to please God at all times, even when they face obstacles, setbacks and rejection. God guides and sustains those who He calls – those who accept their call can, therefore, be fearless in the face of adversity.

If you are not yet fulfilling your call, I hope the call stories in this chapter and the previous chapter will inspire you to live your call. The people around you have needs. If you notice their needs, ask yourself whether you have the skills, aptitudes, experience or resources to respond. If you notice a problem, you could be the solution to it. Maybe that is the reason why you notice it in the first place! If you feel an inner urge or a stirring in your heart, this may be God speaking to you about your call. As I pointed out in Chapter Two, we have a *God Positioning System* within us to guide us through life. We need to pray and listen to God for instructions. Don't ignore His voice when He stirs your heart. Respond with obedience and faith. God will do the rest.

When you serve others, you are also serving God. And those who serve God with the gifts that He has given them find favour with Him. Like the people whose call journeys I have reviewed in this chapter, you will feel a sense of peace, fulfilment, bliss, personal growth and *'aliveness'*. Although the journey will have twists and turns, you will end up exactly where God wants you to be, doing the things you were created to do. You will have the satisfaction of arriving at your destination knowing that you have fulfilled God's mission on earth.

END OF CHAPTER QUESTIONS

- What skills and talents has God given to you?
- How are you using the gifts and talents that God has given to you?
- What do you feel called to do?
- Do you trust God to guide you through your call?
- If you are not living your call, what is preventing you from fulfilling it?

Chapter Five

Hearing God's Call

"The value of persistent prayer is not that He will hear us but that we will finally hear Him."   Unknown

God is constantly speaking to us, even though we are often unaware of His overtures. He wants to talk to us about His plans for our lives and the mission to which He has called us. Throughout the Bible, He uses a variety of ways to call His people. He still calls people today in the same way as He did then and values them equally. This chapter looks at how we can hear and discern God's call. It also explains how we can distinguish between God's voice and other voices.

INTRODUCTION

We have so far established that everyone was made for a purpose and calling. We have also demonstrated that God calls everyone. Some of us are still waiting to hear God's call and are wondering how to hear from Him. Some expect to hear an audible voice calling their name, perhaps an experience such as the way God called young Samuel or the way He called Moses by name through the 'burning bush' or Saul while he was on the way to Damascus.

While God has the power to call us audibly by name and give us our assignment, we should recognise that God is not limited to one mode of communication. God has a variety of ways of communicating with us. This is clear from Scriptures. We have seen how God used different methods to communicate with those whom He called in Biblical times. When God calls us to duty, He uses the medium of communication which is appropriate for us to hear Him. His call is unmistakably clear. We often hear but we sometimes ignore the voice and run away like Jonah.

YOUR RELATIONSHIP WITH GOD

God is a benevolent and personal God. He wants to have a personal relationship with each of us. We will miss God's call if we neglect to have a relationship with Him or if we choose not to listen. When we have a relationship with someone, we get to know their voice and how best to communicate with them. Our communication options increase depending on the closeness of the type of relationship we have with others. I have friends whom I am able to communicate with without uttering a single word. I am able to use a variety of non-verbal communication. I understand their gestures, postures, physiology, eye movements and even their thoughts. They would start a sentence and I am able to complete it. I am able to do this because I have a very close relationship with these friends. This is obviously not possible with strangers or even with those who are casual friends.

In John 10, Jesus made a similar point. He describes His relationship with His followers as akin to that of a 'shepherd and his sheep'.

> *"The gatekeeper opens the gate... and the sheep listen to His voice. He calls His own sheep by name and leads them out. When He has brought out all his own, He goes on ahead of them, and His sheep follow him because they know His voice. But they will never follow a stranger; in fact, they will run away from Him because they do not recognize a stranger's voice."*
>
> John 10:3–5

Jesus said *"My sheep listen to my voice; I know them, and they follow me"* (John 10:27). When Jesus said 'my sheep', He is referring to those who have a relationship with Him. These people are His sheep. They are the ones who are more likely to hear and recognise His call because they have a relationship with Him. They know His voice and are able to distinguish between their Shepherd's voice and the voice of others.

Anyone can have a relationship with God. We are made in God's image and this makes it natural for us to connect with Him. We need to acknowledge His existence and His attributes of omniscience, omnipotence and omnipresence. God did not just create us and then disappear. He wants to have an active relationship with us and is constantly reaching out to us, even though some of us may not be aware of His overtures. He regularly sends us messages through a variety of ways, and they often go unnoticed.

I do not believe we need to communicate with God through a third party as is widely claimed in some religious faiths. We are all created equally and every one of us has equal access to God, our Creator. We do not need permission from a religious master or special agent to communicate with God. He is always available to us. Some theologians say we must first repent of our 'sins' and 'be born again' before we can have a relationship with God. Christianity is based on this doctrine. Bishop Desmond Tutu reminds us that *"God is not a Christian"*. He is the God of everyone – sinners, saints, people of all faiths and every walk of life. No one is excluded.

If we accept God and develop an active, trusting and loving relationship with Him we can hear when He calls us. The deeper our relationship with Him, the more we will hear from Him and experience miracles in our life.

We should strive to have a deep and consistent relationship with God at all times. All too often many of us forget about Him when things are going well in our lives, and seek Him in times of crisis. In such moments of desperation to hear His voice, we may feel frustrated with His apparent slowness in responding to our requests. We may even find ourselves questioning whether He still communicates as He did during Biblical times.

I also break company with those who believe that we must

practice religious rituals and other rigid formulas before we can hear from God. In some religions like Hinduism and Buddhism, people use yoga and other meditation exercises to 'find' God. Christians, Muslims and Jews have developed their own rules to know God. These include following a strict dress code, chanting prescribed mantras and other rituals.

God is more interested in the state of our heart and our willingness to develop a close relationship with Him than religious practices. He is interested in us as we are. All He expects of us is humility and a willingness to faithfully obey His call.

Each of us is valued equally. There is nothing we can do to distinguish ourselves from others in order to gain more favour from God. Putting on ceremonial and medieval-style robes won't earn us any brownie points with God. Praying for hours each day with a pious countenance won't push us up in the pecking order. With God, there is no hierarchy, patronage system or favouritism.

We all have His ear and He is reaching out constantly to all of us with His plans for our lives.

> *"For I know the plans I have for you, declares the Lord, plans to prosper you and not to harm you, plans to give you hope and a future."* Jeremiah 29:11

He has a plan for all of us regardless of our gender, ethnicity, culture, nationality, faith, sexual orientation, material status, disability, health status, or personal circumstances.

WAYS OF HEARING FROM GOD

God is a God of variety and this is even seen in the different ways that He communicates with us. Many people expect Him to speak to them audibly as He spoke with Adam in the Garden of Eden or Moses in the 'burning bush' or young Samuel in the middle of the night. Yes, He can speak to you this way if He chooses. But He has other ways of speaking to you too. We should not think that speaking to you audibly and directly is better than the other ways. Not every one of us will hear from Him in this way.

We use different means to communicate with each other, depending on what we think is appropriate and effective at the time. Why shouldn't we expect the same from God? I communicate with my three-year old great-granddaughter differently from how I communicate with my 25-year-old granddaughter. I speak audibly to the baby or use non-verbal communication to get her attention. Writing a letter to the baby or sending a text or emailing her would be less effective.

GOD SPEAKS AUDIBLY

Adam, Noah, Abraham, Moses, Samuel, Job and many others were called directly by God. Can this still happen today? The answer is a categorical yes. We often read about people who reported that God has spoken audibly to them and engaged in full-blown conversations lasting hours. In fact, this is the subject of a bestselling trilogy of books by Neal Donald Walsch – *see Conversations with God – An Uncommon Dialogue* (Books 1, 2, and 3).

At the time, Walsch was experiencing a series of setbacks in his life when he decided to write an angry letter to God to vent his frustrations. Much to his surprise, God provided an audible and direct response to each of his angry questions. In Walsh's words, after noting all his questions, he heard a voice over his right shoulder say:

> *"Do you really want an answer to all these questions or are you just venting?"* Interview – Neale Donald Walsch on CNS's Larry King Live, 7 April 2000

His trilogy of books is a transcription of the answers that he claimed to have received from God. This helped him to transform his life spiritually and materially. The first volume of *Conversations with God* remained on the *New York Times* Bestseller List for 135 weeks and has been translated into 37 languages.

Walsch's experience is not unusual. Almost 600 years ago, Joan of Arc claimed to hear God's voice calling her to save her people. From age 13, she claimed to hear God speaking to her with messages in her native French language. These conversations were regular and, after a while, occurred at will. She often heard the voice after the ringing of the Church bell. Whilst some people believed her claims, others thought they were the result of hallucinations or some type of mental health problem. She was burnt at the stake in 1431 and died a martyr's death for her witness.

I can attest to hearing the voice of God. I remember attending a ceremony in St Paul's Cathedral in London. I was sitting with some friends whilst the ceremony was in progress. All of a sudden, I found myself in a trance-like state and I found it hard to keep my eyes open and focus on the proceedings. Whilst I was 'half-awake and half-asleep', I heard a voice speaking to me. It was a command to return to Burundi to start a community development project. The voice reassured me that I should go on this mission with courage because all my needs would be taken care of. I can vividly recall hearing the words *"I will be with you from start to finish. You do not need a partner. I will provide for all your needs."*

When I emerged from the trance, I was visibly shaken. I shared my experience with my friends who were seated with me. I realised that God had called me unmistakably to serve the people in Burundi. At the time of writing, I am in the process of making plans to return to Burundi to start this work. Two years prior to this experience in St Paul's Cathedral, I made my first visit to Burundi as part of a Church of England delegation. God clearly wants me to do further service in this remote part of the world which would not normally be on my travelling list. Many people find stories of this kind to be farfetched. A common reaction is to dismiss them as figments of the imagination or some kind of mental health problem. However, experiences such as the one that I had in St Paul's Cathedral are quite common, especially for people who have a personal relationship with God.

GOD SPEAKS THROUGH OUR DREAMS AND VISIONS

Some of us will hear from God in other ways. He may use dreams and visions to call us to our assignments. God never breaks His promises:

> *"And afterward, I will pour out my Spirit on all people. Your sons and daughters will prophesy, your old men will dream dreams, your young men will see visions."*
>
> Joel 2:28

There are many examples in the Bible of God calling people through visions and dreams. Daniel and other prophets had dreams and visions. Abraham received his call through a vision. With Joseph, God went even further. Apart from revealing His plan to Joseph through dreams, God also gave him the gift of interpreting dreams. Joseph famously interpreted Pharaoh's dream and found favour with him. God's plan was to use Joseph to prepare the Egyptians and the Israelites to cope with a devastating famine which lasted for seven years. We also saw that, apart from speaking audibly to young Samuel, God prepared him for his call with dreams and visions. God used dreams to point out the wrongdoings of Eli's sons and the judgement which will be inflicted on Eli's household. Samuel obeyed and conveyed the message to Eli.

In the New Testament, we also see many accounts of God using dreams and visions to speak to His people. For example, dreams played a major role in the announcement of Jesus' own calling. We are told *"an angel of the Lord appeared to [Joseph] in a dream"* (*see* Matthew 1:20). Without the assurance of this dream, one suspects Joseph would have chosen to separate from Mary on grounds of infidelity. After the child was born, God appeared again to Joseph to tell him to seek refuge with his family in Egypt as Herod was plotting to kill the baby. When Herod died, he was summoned in a dream to return home.

God continues to use dreams and visions to speak to people today about their call. Let us consider two examples. America's first black millionaire owed her fortune to a dream. Sarah Breedlove (1867–1919), better known as Madam C. J. Walker, is cited in *The Guinness Book of Records* as the first American female self-made millionaire. Walker suffered from a common scalp infection which caused hair loss. She tried different medicines and hair products to cure the problem, but to no avail.

This was to change when she had a dream about what African herbs she was to mix and apply to her scalp. The remedy was a success and she went on to establish Madam C. J. Walker Manufacturing Company to manufacture and distribute a line of beauty and hair products for black women. She became one of the wealthiest and most successful female entrepreneurs of her time.

There are countless other present–day examples of people

who have received guidance from God about their call through dreams. About a year ago, I was attracted to the title of a book with the caption *The Wonderful You — Find Your Purpose and Live the Life of Your Dreams Now.* As I browsed the opening pages of the book, I was intrigued by the author's story. Following a catalogue of adversities, his life hit rock-bottom and he found himself burdened by debt and poor mental health. His long-term relationship with his fiancée had ended and he had lost his high-profile job and virtually all of his life savings in a business deal that went wrong.

He recounted his difficulties in bouncing back from these setbacks. Nothing seemed to work. Then, out of the blue, he had a dream one night about what to do to reverse his setbacks. He was instructed in the dream to forgive the people who had betrayed him. Through the dream, he was also provided with a brief for writing a self-help book, as well as a business idea. He complied with the instructions in the dream and before long went on to experience a profound transformation of his life at all levels. He now enjoys financial security, peace of mind and personal fulfilment from living out another phase in his call.

When we are asleep, the noise or 'monkey chatter' that normally pervades our minds cease. This is a good time for God to get our attention as there is little noise to drown out His voice. In our sleeping state, we are also more receptive to whatever God tells us. There is less resistance and less questioning of His message.

GOD SPEAKS THROUGH OUR EXPERIENCE

God also speaks to us through our experiences. Our experiences are not random, haphazard events. Sometimes this is the only way God can get our attention. Some of us need a wake-up call before we can pay attention to God's subtle call.

Jonah learned about God's call through a series of dramatic experiences. These include a raging storm and being swallowed in the belly of a huge fish. Job's catastrophic losses were a part of his call. Today, his name is synonymous with faith. In spite of the loss of his health, wealth and members of his family, he did not lose faith in God. God used him to teach us what is possible when we stay obedient to Him in times of adversity. He helps us to overcome the storm and compensates us for our losses. The Bible tells us that Job was more prosperous in the second half of his life than in the first half.

We also see how God communicated with Joseph through his experiences. His position in his household, relationship with his father, humiliation at the hands of his brothers, enslavement and imprisonment were all part of his call. God used these experiences to prepare him to be Pharaoh's Second-in-command and to save His people from famine and starvation. Joseph told his brothers:

> *"You intended to harm me, but God intended it for good to accomplish what is now being done, the saving of many lives."* Genesis 50:2

Nothing can happen to us without God's permission. God uses our experiences to build our character and to strengthen others. We are all blessed and empowered by the experiences of those who have overcome difficult trials and tests like Joseph, Job and Paul. When we look back on our lives after we have been through the storms of life, we see the purpose and meaning behind our experiences. Those who adopted the right attitude and response invariable emerge stronger, better, more fulfilled and having a deeper relationship with God. In the end, they realise there were hidden blessings and opportunities within their trials.

God speaks to us and develops us through our experiences. When you are called by Him, you should expect to be tested. It will never be plain sailing. It is His way of preparing you to be the person He wants you to be. That is the only way you can fulfil your divine assignment. In Jesus' words:

> *"Then He said to them all: 'Whoever wants to be my disciple must deny themselves and take up their cross daily and follow me'."* Luke 9:23

Your experiences, both positive and negative, are a part of your calling. If you are not faced with difficult tests and trials, you are not experiencing great growth. Great calls come with difficult challenges and hard conversations with God.

GOD SPEAKS THROUGH SCRIPTURE

God's words are recorded in various sacred texts. As He is the God of everyone, He has made His message universally acceptable in a variety of media. The Bible is just one of many books where His words are written. The message in these books is strikingly similar. It is a message of love, peace, hope, justice and fulfilment.

It is said that the words written in sacred texts like the Bible and Quran are God-breathed. It is God's message to us. It takes on life and personal meaning when we read and meditate on the Word of God. Through His Word, God will provide us with guidance on all aspects of our personal calling. We are told that:

> *"the word of God is alive and active. Sharper than any double-edged sword, it penetrates even to dividing soul and spirit, joints and marrow; it judges the thoughts and attitudes of the heart."*   Hebrews 4:12

A friend of mine explained how God directed him to use Scripture to help a grief-stricken colleague. The man's wife ended their relationship, threw him out of the house and left him with nothing. My friend found him wandering on the street in despair. As the distraught man began to talk about his abandonment by his wife, my friend recalled how he heard the words from Psalms 27 echoing in his mind:

"Though my father and mother forsake me, the Lord will receive me." Psalms 27:4

He was led by an inner voice to use these words to encourage his colleague to accept the loss of his wife. He reminded the man that even parents sometimes abandon their children. If this is possible in a parent/child relationship, he should not be surprised or shocked by his wife's actions. With these words, the man was able to put his loss into perspective and was ready to move on with his life.

On numerous occasions, I have been directed by a quiet voice within me to read particular verses or chapters from God's Word to help me through difficult circumstances. As I read and meditate on God's Word, I often gain answers to questions and feel God's loving and calming presence in my life. Each time I read particular sections of the Bible, I receive new insights. It is like having a different conversation with someone each time we meet.

GOD SPEAKS THROUGH OTHER PEOPLE

In Biblical times, God called some people through messengers and angels. For example, He sent angels to communicate with Joseph and Mary. Nowadays, we do not have to wait for anything as dramatic as this. We often hear God communicating with us through the words or actions of other people.

Have you ever had the experience of listening to a talk, sermon, song, poem or a simple throw-away remark by someone which speaks to your heart or sheds light on a problem that you have been struggling to solve? This is a good example of God speaking to you through messengers. We all have moments like this, although we may not attach any importance to them.

- Have you ever been touched by the bonding and love displayed by children at play?
- Have you ever found yourself in awe from an act of kindness from a stranger?
- Have you ever been moved to pray or act by the concerns of others?

Perhaps it may be a reaction to something you read about or come across in the news. These are all examples of God speaking to us through other people.

GOD SPEAKS THROUGH NATURE

We can experience God's voice in nature. God may use the changes in the climate and seasons to remind us that challenges in our lives are natural and inevitable. Some days it may be sunny and other days it may be wet and cloudy. When we see a beautiful rainbow, God may send a thought or impression to our minds that we cannot have rainbows without rain.

For those of us who are impatient about our call and goals, God may use nature to teach us about the virtue of patience. Everything is accomplished in nature when the time is right. There is no force or struggle in nature. The sun shines without force. A flower blooms without force. A bird flies without force. Everything in nature flows effortlessly.

God uses the heavy winds and the crashing waves against the shore to remind us of His existence and omnipotence. God is communicating with us through everything we see in the natural world. That is one of the reasons why artists, inventors and other people normally turn to nature in their quest for solutions to problems, new ideas and inspiration. As they pose their questions in this natural environment and listen with obedience, God invariably reveals Himself and engages in a dialogue with them. This often leads to practical ideas and inspired solutions – a sure sign that God is party to these conversations.

OTHER WAYS OF HEARING FROM GOD

I have discussed some of the ways God communicates with us. God is a God of variety and is constantly finding new ways of communicating with us. As our Creator, He delights in finding creative ways of communicating with us. He will manifest Himself differently to every one of us with a different form and style of communication.

God's nature makes His communication forms and styles different from ours. They are certainly more versatile and creative. In scripture, we have seen how He communicates through a 'storm'.

"Then the Lord spoke to Job out of the storm."

Job 38:1

In Exodus 19:18, God communicated with Moses through 'fire' and 'smoke'. We have seen how God has even communicated with those whom He called through a 'donkey':

> *"Then the Lord opened the donkey's mouth, and it said to Balaam, 'What have I done to you to make you beat me these three times?"* Numbers 22:28

He spoke to Elijah in a still, small voice:

> *"After the earthquake came a fire, but the LORD was not in the fire. And after the fire came a gentle whisper."*

1 Kings 19:12

This method of hearing from God is a variation on an audible and direct voice. Research undertaken by psychological anthropologist Professor Tanya Marie Luhrmann, author of *When God Talks Back: Understanding the American Evangelical Relationship with God,* concludes that hearing from God 'in a quiet voice' or through images is quite common. Professor Luhrmann writes:

"For the last ten years, I have been doing anthropological and psychological research among experientially oriented evangelicals, the sort of people who seek a personal relationship with God and who expect that God will talk back. For most of them, most of the time, God talks back in a quiet voice they hear inside their minds, or through images that come to mind during prayer. But many of them also reported sensory experiences of God." See http://religion.blogs.cnn.com/2012/12/29/my-take-if-you-hear-god-speak-audibly-you-usually-arent-crazy/

God can speak to you through anything or anyone you see and experience in your surroundings during your daily routine. You should develop a mindset where you naturally expect to hear from God, no matter where you are or what you may be doing. Listen to what thoughts flow to your mind or your reaction to what you see, hear, feel or perceive through your whole being. Unlike humans who speak to your ears, God speaks to your whole being. He speaks past your ears, straight to your heart. He uses anyone and everything to achieve His purpose.

RECOGNISING GOD'S VOICE

God's omnipotence and omniscience make it possible for Him to communicate with us in an infinite number of ways. His voice may be loud, strong, firm, extraordinary, gentle, quiet, ordinary, soothing, loving, witty, mysterious, miraculous, purposeful, perfectly timed and distinctive. Once you hear it, you will know it. It is impossible to confuse it with your ego or some other external voice. More commonly, God speaks to us through 'inner promptings' from the Holy Spirit. His message will leave a clear and unmistakable impression on our hearts, not our ears. When Jesus was resurrected, He met two of His disciples on the road to Emmaus and spoke to them. The disciples explained the effect this had on their hearts:

> *"Were not our hearts burning within us while he talked with us on the road and opened the Scriptures to us?"*
>
> Luke 24:32

The Holy Spirit stirs us to do good deeds and to see the best in ourselves and others.

When you are able to see the beauty in others, you can be sure that God is guiding you and is communicating with you. If you are guided to make a decision and you feel peace instead of turmoil, this is a sign that you are guided by God and that you have made the right decision. God will never tell you to hurt anyone or do anything that contradicts His Word as written in the Bible and other sacred books. We know that

> *"All Scripture is God-breathed and is useful for teaching, rebuking, correcting and training in righteousness."*
>
> 2 Timothy 3:16

If you find yourself judging or criticising others, you are clearly not following God's voice. God reminds us in Scripture that we should not judge others. If you find yourself feeling fearful or doubting yourself, again this is not God. If you hear a voice telling you that you are not good enough, this is not God's voice. God's Word tells us we should not fear anything or anyone. It tells us we should love ourselves and that all things are possible. If you find yourself feeling vindictive or harbouring any negative emotions towards anyone or yourself, this is not coming from God. These behaviours are not consistent with God's nature. God is a loving, benevolent and forgiving God. He is a God of possibilities and opportunities. What He tells us to do or say reflects His nature.

In contrast, when you feel inspired to help someone, then this is God clearly speaking to your heart or conscience. When you find yourself using your natural talents and following your passions, you will know that this is God speaking to you and guiding you. When you tune in to God's message, you will naturally offer your seat to the elderly or disabled person who needs it. You will spontaneously open the door for someone and engage in acts of kindness. You will naturally pray for help for those who are in need, rather than speaking unkindly about them. You will forgive those who betray you. You may be led to visit or contact that person who is faced with some crisis and desperately needs help. You will express gratitude for the blessings in your life. When you see someone experiencing ill health, God will use this to remind you of the blessing of health in your life. And you will remember all the ways in which God has answered your prayers and helped you over the years to overcome challenges and setbacks. God has done miraculous things for many people, but they have been too busy to notice.

If you have the right relationship with God and are prepared to listen carefully, you will know His voice. When God called young Samuel, He was not yet spiritually mature to know God's voice. Samuel had to rely on Eli, his teacher, to know that it was God who was calling him. As Samuel's relationship with God grew, he was able to hear and trust God's voice. He was able to hear from God on a regular basis and was prepared to act on God's instructions. This made him become one of Israel's greatest prophets.

A personal and faithful relationship with God will make us feel God's presence and receive wisdom, guidance and power from Him. It will ensure we do not rely on our own wisdom or allow ourselves to be distracted from our call.

OBEDIENCE TO GOD'S CALL

God expects us to be obedient to His call. We should respond with courage even if we do not feel fully equipped to accomplish the task He has for us.

Interestingly, when we study the call stories in the Bible we notice that many of those who were called resisted the call at first. They put forward all kinds of excuses for not heeding the call. These ranged from feelings of inadequacy to questions of inopportune timing.

Moses' example is typical. When God called him in the 'burning bush' to deliver Israel from slavery in Egypt, he was reluctant to accept his commission. His first thought was that he was not worthy of such a call. As he puts it:

> *"Who am I that I should go to Pharaoh and bring the Israelites out of Egypt?"*   Exodus 3:11

God assured him that He will be with him. However, this was not enough for Moses. He came up with another question:

> *"Suppose I go to the Israelites and say to them, 'The God of your fathers has sent me to you,' and they ask me, 'What is his name?' Then what shall I tell them?"*
>   Exodus 3:13

God told him to tell them *"I am who I am"* has sent you. Note *"I am"* is another name for God – the God of Abraham, Isaac and Jacob, the God of your fathers (*see* Exodus 3:15).

Moses hesitated further and asked:

> *"What if they do not believe me or listen to me and say, 'The Lord did not appear to you'?"*   Exodus 4:1

God answered his question with characteristic patience. He told Moses He will perform a number of miracles in the presence of the Israelites to prove that He had sent him to free them from oppression.

This still was not enough for Moses. He came up with a new excuse. He called attention to his speech impediment:

> *"Pardon your servant, Lord. I have never been eloquent, neither in the past nor since you have spoken to your servant. I am slow of speech and tongue."*
>
> Exodus 4:10

God provided yet more reassurance, but this still did not put Moses at complete ease. In Exodus 4:13, he pleaded to God: *"Pardon your servant, Lord. Please send someone else."* In the end, God sent Moses' brother, Aaron, to help him carry out the task of leading the Israelites from Egypt to the land which He had promised Abraham. Aaron acted as his mouthpiece and deputy.

Some people even miss their call due to utter disobedience. The Gospel of Luke narrates Jesus' encounter with a rich young ruler. This man wanted to become one of Jesus' disciples and asked Jesus what were the requirements for becoming one of His followers. Jesus told him to sell his possessions and give to the poor to fulfil His requirements (Luke 18:22). This was too great a sacrifice to make. We are told:

> *"When he heard this, he became very sad, because he was a man of great wealth."*
>
> Luke 18:23

Many of us react like Moses and the rich young ruler when God calls us. I reacted in the same way when God called me to bring justice and practical help to asylum-seekers. I resisted the call, but God negated every excuse I devised. By way of illustration, let me say a bit more about how my call experience unfolded.

For many years I was employed in social work and three other roles. I had plans to retire at age 60 and did just that as soon as I turned 60. What I did not know at the time is that God had other plans for my life. Shortly after my retirement, a friend drew my attention to a job opportunity with The Rainbow Project in Nottingham. There were two strands to the job – promoting racial and cultural diversity, and providing advocacy, practical and spiritual support to asylum-seekers. I knew a lot about the first strand but very little about the second.

At first, I had no interest whatsoever in the role. My focus was my retirement and the life of leisure I was looking forward to in the sunny Caribbean after working for over 40 years. However, my friend insisted that I was ideal for the role. I resisted in vain. She nagged me constantly. She had a solution for every objection I raised. Reluctantly, I decided to apply for the post.

Judging from what transpired during the application and selection process, I have absolutely no doubt that the job was God-sent and was a part of my call. First, I missed the deadline for submitting my application. As there was a postal strike, the recruiters decided to accept a late application. The interview was a success. However, I was unable to take up the post straightaway. My father was gravely ill and I chose to travel to New York to spend time with him. At this point, my recruiters offered to wait for up to nine months for me to take up the post. I could not believe my ears. By this point, I was convinced I would not succeed in talking myself out of this job. No matter what I said or did, the organisation was accommodating. In the end, I went to New York and returned two months later to take up the post.

I served in this role for almost ten years until I retired at the age of 70. While I have enjoyed all the roles that I have assumed over the course of my working life, this job was probably my most fulfilling. Some of my achievements in the role were miraculous.

Experiences like these remind me that we need to do more to let God tell us what He wants us to do, rather than doing what we find easy. We also need to avoid drowning out God's voice with our negative thoughts. All too often, the noise from our own voice can make it hard for us to hear God's voice or follow His call. Self-doubt, fear, and low self-esteem can cause us to disobey the assignment that God wants us to undertake for others and for His glory.

We should accept God's call with passion and conviction. King David provides a very good example of this. During his setbacks and challenges, he reminds us:

> "Even though I walk through the darkest valley, I will fear no evil, for you are with me; your rod and your staff, they comfort me." Psalm 23:4

CONCLUDING REMARKS

God is constantly communicating with us, whether or not we are aware of it. He wants to tell us about His call for our lives and guide us through it. He wants to work in partnership with us to make the world a better place for ourselves and others. If we listen, we can all hear His voice. He will speak to us through whatever medium resonates with us. Throughout the Bible, we see Him communicating with His people through direct and audible instructions, dreams, visions, His Word, nature, angels, messengers, other people, music, prayer, miracles, events, experiences, thoughts, and intuition, the still small voice within us, our conscience, and a myriad of other ways. He is a God of infinite possibilities. He is not limited in what He does or how He does them.

If we develop a close relationship with God and listen actively, we are more likely to hear when He speaks with us. Like young Samuel, when we hear His voice, we should be obedient and our only response should be, *"Speak, Lord, for your servant is listening"*. We do not have to do anything great to know God. Simply listening, trusting and acting on what God is saying to us is enough to please God. Each day, get into the habit of finding quality time to listen to what God is telling you. The quieter you are, the more you will hear.

END OF CHAPTER QUESTIONS

- Can you hear God communicating with you?
- How does He communicate with you?
- What is He calling you to do?
- Are you ready and willing to say *"Speak, Lord, for your servant is listening?"*

Chapter Six

Ten Barriers to Hearing God's Voice

*"Call to me and I will answer you and tell you great
and unsearchable things you do not know."*

Jeremiah 33:3

In the previous chapter, I looked at how God speaks
to us. In this chapter, I will discuss ten common
barriers that can prevent us from hearing God's voice
and following His will. I will also offer practical
guidance to help you better tune in to God's voice.
God is constantly speaking to us to offer comfort,
encouragement, strength, lessons, correction, guidance
and instruction. We run the risk of missing our call, and
struggling through it, if we do not listen attentively to
what He is telling us.

INTRODUCTION

God wants to communicate with you personally about your call. In fact, He is constantly communicating with you about everything that concerns your call. If we listen to Him, He will guide us throughout our call journey. In Proverbs 3:15, we are reminded to *"Trust in the Lord with all our heart, and lean not on our own understanding: in all your ways acknowledge Him, and He shall direct our paths"*.

If you are having problems hearing God's voice, this could be due to one or more of the factors which I will discuss in this chapter. As well as discussing some common barriers to hearing God's voice, I will also discuss how we can overcome them and become better listeners.

POOR LISTENING

Are you really listening? Listening is a skill. Few of us have this skill. In our everyday conversations with our peers, family and members of the public we often speak without actively listening to what others have to say. Some of us may as well speak to ourselves. Others speak but we do not listen. Rather than listening actively to understand what is being said, we wait for the earliest opportunity to jump in to speak. In some cases, we are busy thinking about how we might respond rather than concentrating on what the other party has to say. We act as though no one else has anything interesting to say other than ourselves.

We know someone is not actively listening to us when we notice they are:

- speaking excessively;
- rushing to speak before we have even finished our sentence;
- distracted by something physical or psychological;
- looking away from us (e.g. looking at their watch);
- failing to follow what we have to say;
- failing to seek clarification or additional information about the topic under discussion;
- failing to show empathy or interest in the subject; or
- treating us with disrespect, as though what we have to say does not matter.

If we want to hear God's voice, we should learn to listen to Him actively and treat Him with utmost respect. What God has to say to us is far more important than what we have to say to Him. Listening is a skill. Like all other skills, it can be developed. Get into the habit of consciously and actively listening to God.

The price of not listening to God can be costly. You may miss your call if you don't listen to what God has to say to you. You may find yourself making decisions that lead you down blind alleys. You may fail to hear the answer to your questions or prayers. Some of us will even find ourselves making the same costly mistakes without ever learning from them. Through communication and our obedience to Him, God wants to guide us, teach us, encourage us and correct us so that we can become the best version of ourselves.

PHYSICAL DISTRACTIONS AND NOISE

Some of us may be good listeners but may not be able to hear God's voice because of physical distractions and noise. In Chapter Five, I pointed out that one of the ways God speaks to us is through a gentle whisper or prompting. We read in 1 Kings 19:12 that this was how God spoke, for example, to Elijah: *"After the earthquake came a fire, but the Lord was not in the fire. And after the fire came a gentle whisper."*

We need to be aware of the things that may be drowning out God's voice. Take stock of your life and judge for yourself whether you are living it in a manner that is conducive to hearing from God. We live in an age where there are many things to distract us from listening to God. Many of us are too busy to listen to God. We are busy with work, chasing money, relationships, family life, hobbies and daily routine. On top of these, many are distracted by mobile telephones, social media, video games, magazines, newspapers, peer pressure, keeping up with the Jones' or the Kardashian's and television. Stress and other emotional conditions also play their part. It is hard to hear God's voice when we are overwhelmed by anxiety, worry and the cares of daily life.

We should add distractions from the world to this list. Jesus warned about this in the Parable of the Sower and the Soils:

> *"The one who received the seed that fell among the thorns is the man who hears the word, but the worries of this life and the deceitfulness of wealth choke it, making it unfruitful."*   Matthew 13:22

The 'seed' is God's voice or word. If we are too busy chasing wealth or pre-occupied with the cares of the world, God's word will not be heard.

- Are you one of those people who are too busy to listen to God or to anyone for that matter?
- Are you constantly watching television and spending time on your telephone, video games or computer?
- Do you set aside quiet time to listen actively to God?
- Are you aware of the different ways God may use to speak to you and are you always listening for His voice?

Our challenge is to make our life quiet so that we can hear God's voice. This comes with practice. We need to find time to notice the distractions before we can act to remove them. Once we quiet our mind and start to listen with intent and expectation, we are ready to hear from God.

DISTRACTIONS FROM OTHERS

We sometimes allow our employers, managers, relatives, friends and other significant people in our life to distract us from hearing God's voice. We are often too eager to please these people, even if it means displeasing ourselves and God. Our only obligation should be to please God. Paul writes:

> *"Am I now trying to win the approval of human beings, or of God? Or am I trying to please people? If I were still trying to please people, I would not be a servant of Christ."*
> Galatians 1:10

Few of us have the courage to stand up for what we believe in. We like to play things safe as we are afraid of criticisms and reprisals from those who wield power over us. In one of my job roles, I can remember being derisively labelled as a 'loose cannon' by one of my managers because of my refusal to be distracted from my call. The more I was criticised, the more determined I was to do the work that I knew God was calling me to do. Eventually, I was encouraged to take early retirement. I prayed about the decision to retire and God assured me that it was time to move to new pastures. I had already achieved what God wanted me to get out of this role. This book would not have been written without the benefit of the insights gained from working in the organisation in question.

RELIGION AS A BARRIER

The practices of the church can be a barrier to hearing God's voice and to developing a close relationship with Him. Some churches teach that there is only one true religion. They promote the view that we cannot hear God's voice unless we belong to the right faith and meticulously follow the church's creed and rituals.

This is clearly a false teaching. Religion was founded by man, not God. God transcends religion and all artificial institutions created by society to separate people. Jesus did not come to earth to teach or spread Christianity. He came as an act of love and to be a Light into the world. Through His example, He taught us how to live with each other and to glorify God.

Contrary to the teachings of many religions, we do not have to follow rigid formulas or medieval rituals to enter into a close and loving relationship with God. We do not even have to go to church, as God is present everywhere and readily available to us at all times. I know many people who go to church out of habit rather than to truly serve God. I also know many people who have never visited church but who have a very close relationship with God.

Jesus was very critical of religious leaders while He was on earth. Like many of today's church leaders, they were preoccupied with rituals and symbolic displays of their piety. He observed that:

> *"Everything they do is done for people to see: They make their phylacteries wide and the tassels on their garments long; they love the place of honour at banquets and the most important seats in the synagogues; they love to be greeted with respect in the marketplaces and to be called 'Rabbi' by others."*   Matthew 23:5–7

It is not what we do in church on the Sabbath that matters. It is not what we wear, what we give or how much time we spend singing and praying. It is the quality of our ongoing, daily relationship with God that counts. If we only eat and drink one day a week, we cannot expect to be healthy and well nourished. By the same token, we would be spiritually malnourished if we don't nurture and build our relationship with God on a constant and ongoing basis.

FAILURE TO RECOGNISE GOD'S VOICE

In John 10:27, Jesus says *"My sheep listen to my voice; I know them, and they follow me"*. To hear and know God's voice, you need to be one of his 'sheep'. In this wonderful metaphor, God is our Shepherd and those who have a relationship with Him are His sheep. Sheep know their master's voice and obey every command. This is generally true of other animals. Cats, dogs, horses and other animals respond to their carers' voice.

Unless we have a close relationship with God, we will not recognise His voice when He speaks to us. We may pray about something and receive the answer without knowing that our prayer has been answered. As we saw in Chapter Five, the answer may not always be audible. God may answer us in a myriad of different forms. The answer to what we pray about or what God wants us to do may come in the form of images, signs, conversations or messages from other people, our personal experiences, and so on. If you are inattentive or stray away from God like a lost sheep, you will miss the Shepherd's message.

I remember attending church one Sunday and heard God telling me to give the £60 that I had in my purse to a stranger in the congregation. On my way to church that day, I felt guided to withdraw £60 from the cash machine. I was planning to use a portion of this for offering and the rest for petrol. During the service, I heard a voice telling me to give the £60 to the stranger instead of using it the way I had intended. I waited until after the service and discreetly offered the money to the woman. I felt embarrassed as I did not know the woman and was not sure how she would react to my gesture. She took the money, thanked me and walked away. A few weeks later when she next saw me, she walked up to me and thanked me again. She told me that God had used me to answer her prayer. Her rent was due the following day and she was short of exactly £60 and had no means of finding it.

Whenever I share this story with people, some of them react with disbelief. One man even asked me: how did God speak to you? In what language did He speak with you and with what accent? Unless you have experienced God's 'voice', this is hard to explain. What I heard was not an audible voice. It is best described as a strong super-imposition of God's Spirit on my mind and heart. It is a very compelling feeling. It is very hard to ignore as it is so deeply etched on your conscience. Although I was left with nothing in my purse on that Sunday, I felt a strong sense of relief and freedom. I knew the voice was God's, not mine, and certainly not the devil's or any other third party. If it were my own voice, I would have argued with myself about the wisdom of giving the whole of my £60 to a stranger when I needed it for other purposes. The devil would certainly not encourage acts of kindness and self-sacrifice. What I was told to do was in line with God's nature. I was in no doubt that I had acted on God's instructions.

Thus, another way to hear God's voice is to become a faithful follower and develop a close relationship with Him.

In this way, you will learn more about Him and how He communicates with you. The more you hear His voice and see His hand in the events of your life, the more you will learn to trust Him and rely on Him to guide you through your call.

WITHHOLDING FORGIVENESS

None of us will go through life without being hurt or betrayed by the actions of others. Hurt and betrayals can take any number of forms – lies, infidelity, criminal damage, financial losses through theft and deceit, insensitive and hurtful criticisms, and other forms of injustice. In such situations, people naturally feel hurt.

Acts of unkindness are clearly not right. However, this is no excuse for not forgiving those who have done us harm. Lack of forgiveness is a major barrier to hearing God's voice. It damages your relationship with God. How can you hear God's voice if you are sizzling with anger, bitterness and a desire for revenge?

An unforgiving heart does not just make it hard to hear God's voice. It also causes harm to your mental and physical health. It puts the body in a state of stress, causes muscles to tighten and undermines the body's immune system. Headaches, insomnia, skin irritations, cancer and increases in blood pressure and cholesterol levels are common consequences of unforgiveness.

Forgiveness is a requirement of your Creator.

"Bear with each other and forgive whatever grievances you may have against one another. Forgive as the Lord forgave you." Colossians 3:13

Paul reminds us in various parts of his writings that we should forgive readily and quickly.

"In your anger do not sin. Do not let the sun go down while you are still angry." Ephesians 4:26

Although it does not come to us naturally, we need to forgive out of obedience to God. Forgiveness leads to freedom from anger, bitterness and resentment. It is in our personal interest as we are the ones who bear the most pain. When Joseph made the decision to forgive his brothers, his life prospered. From being sold into slavery by his jealous brothers, he went on to become the second most powerful man in Egypt next to Pharaoh. If you want God's blessings to flow into your life, you must be willing and ready to forgive those who do you wrong. We are reminded in this well-known quote by Anne Lamott that *"Not forgiving is like drinking rat poison and then waiting for the rat to die"*. It does more harm to you than your offender. Forgiveness is an act of strength and courage. It releases you to truly heed your call and receive God's guidance along your journey.

FAILURE TO LIVE IN THE MOMENT

If we don't live in the moment, it means our mind is somewhere else. It is either preoccupied with things from the past or the future. This suggests we literally miss out on what is happening in the present moment – right here, right now. This is perhaps the worst type of 'mental noise' or 'busyness'. There is simply no silence to hear God or even to see God's invisible hand in what is going on around us.

When we live in the past and the future, negative emotions drown out God's voice. If we dwell in the past, we may find ourselves overwhelmed by feelings of guilt, shame, anger, distress, regret and disappointment. As we think about our mistakes or our experiences, whether good or bad, we can't help saying "if only I had known" or "if only I had pursued another option". Living in the future also paralyses us with negative emotions such as worry and anxiety. It can leave us with feelings of horror as we find ourselves fearing the worse.

I know many people who live their life in this way. Some worry about how they would cope if they lost their job or their spouse. Anxiety causes many to suffer from ill health and self-inflicted stress.

Living in the present is where we can expect to find peace. There are no negative emotions when we live in stillness and in the present. This is where we are most likely to hear God's still, quiet voice. When we live in the present, we accept life as it is, not as it ought to be or could have been. We welcome the present moment with gratitude and without any form of judgement. We now choose to witness our thoughts; we are no longer a prisoner of them. As we declutter our minds and stop 'talking to ourselves', we can now listen to what God has to tell us. Alan Watts summarises the point excellently in a YouTube video:

> *"If we are talking all of the time, we never hear what anyone else has to say. In the same way, if we are talking to ourselves all the time, we are never listening, we have nothing to think about other than thoughts, and are never in relationship with reality."*

SELF-IMPOSED BARRIERS

Self-imposed barriers come in different forms. Some of the more common ones are doubt, false beliefs and poor self-esteem and fear. Let us consider each of these barriers more closely.

DOUBT

For some of us, doubt can be a barrier to hearing from God. How can you hear God's voice if you doubt His existence or any of His attributes? I find it easy to hear from God because of my belief in His existence and what I know about His nature.

In Chapter One and the Epilogue, I made the case for God's existence and looked at His nature. God is active in the world and in our lives. The all-powerful, all-knowing, ever-present, unchanging, merciful and benevolent God is constantly communicating with us. He is interested in every aspect of our life and every decision we make. Nothing we do is too minor to attract His interest. God wants to guide us in all our decisions. If we listen to Him, we will receive the right answer to our questions about the next move in our life. Wouldn't it be good to receive support and guidance from the one with infinite knowledge about us and who knows the answer to the big decisions that we face in life such as:

- Should I change job?
- Should I find a partner or, if you already have one, should I get married now?
- How can I make this relationship work better?
- Should I start a family or have more children?
- Should I join this church or this club?
- Should I pursue this career or apply for this course or this job?
- Should I make this investment?

Whatever stage we are at in our life, and whatever decision we are faced with, God is available, willing and able to help us. If you speak to Him and remove the barrier of doubt, He will provide the right answer to our question, and we will hear it.

FALSE BELIEFS

It is possible to have total belief in God's existence and still not able to hear His voice if we hold false beliefs about how

God works and communicates with us. Over the years, I have heard a number of such beliefs expressed in throw-away lines in conversations with colleagues, friends and family members.

The list includes beliefs such as:

- God only speaks to people who are in ministerial roles or those with spiritual gifts;
- God will not listen to me because of my sins;
- God will only listen to me if I give at least 10% of what I earn in tithe;
- God will not listen to me unless I learn to pray the right way; and
- God is limited in the ways in which He speaks to me.

Although widely held, these are all false beliefs. Let us look at each of these false beliefs in turn.

GOD ONLY SPEAKS TO PEOPLE IN MINISTERIAL ROLES OR THOSE WITH SPIRITUAL GIFTS

This is plainly not true. God creates everyone equally and values everyone the same. He gives every one of us gifts and these gifts are valued equally. All gifts are spiritual when used to do His work on earth. The pathway to God is available to all of us — we do not need to communicate to God via a priest or a person of the cloth as they are often called in the United Kingdom. God wants to have a close and personal relationship with each of us, regardless of our background.

GOD WILL NOT LISTEN TO ME BECAUSE OF MY SINS

This is a false belief, often reinforced by the teachings of many religions. None of us is sinless; this includes people in the ministry. If being sinless was the criterion for hearing God's voice, none of us would be able to hear from God.

> *"As it is written: there is no one righteous, not even one."* Romans 3:10

God wants to have a relationship with everyone, whether they are saints or sinners. If we seek Him, we can find Him. We simply need to listen and obey His instructions. His interactions with us are not based on our righteousness, but on His grace, mercy and benevolence. God will never turn His back on us because of our sins. No matter how grave our misdemeanours, He draws near to us and is ready and willing to forgive us. Our job is simply to let go of our sins and do our best to develop a close relationship with God.

GOD WILL ONLY LISTEN TO ME IF I GIVE 10% OF MY INCOME IN TITHE

Tithe means one-tenth or ten per cent. There is an expectation in many churches that we should donate at least ten per cent of our income to support God's work. Some churches insist on this amount regardless of the person's circumstances. They are made to feel guilty if they don't pay this amount. The false belief is promoted by their leaders that tithing affects people's ability to hear from God and to receive God's favour.

This doctrine is misleading and impractical. Tithing should be voluntary, flexible and reflect a person's circumstances. Paul tells us:

> *"Each of you should give what you have decided in your heart to give, not reluctantly or under compulsion, for God loves a cheerful giver."*   2 Cor. 9:7

If someone is unemployed or does not have sufficient resources to meet essential outgoings, it is unrealistic and irresponsible for the church to expect them to pay ten per cent in tithe under such circumstances.

God's work requires more than money. People should be encouraged to give what they are able to give. Some may be able to tithe in cash, while others may only be able to tithe in kind or simply give their time. When I was in Burundi, I noticed that tithing in cash was the exception rather than the norm. People cheerfully gave their time, labour, skills and goods.

Contrary to what some churches teach, tithing does not affect our capacity to hear from God. God sees our heart and values what we are able to give, regardless of what form this takes. He does not love us more if we tithe in cash or less if we tithe in kind. It does not even matter to Him if we are not able to tithe at all. God gives us a free will. He does not force us to do anything we do not want to do. Regardless of what we give or what we withhold from Him, God will ensure His work is done in the world. We cannot bribe Him to act.

GOD WILL NOT LISTEN TO ME UNLESS I LEARN TO PRAY THE RIGHT WAY

This is patently a false belief. First and foremost, God is interested in the motive behind our prayer. He *"judges the thoughts and attitudes of the heart"* (Hebrews 4:12). God hears our prayers whether we pray aloud or in silence; whether we pray with a stutter or with eloquence; or whether we pray kneeling or standing. He even hears our prayers when we are too confused to pray and overwhelmed by problems. Paul writes in Romans 8:26: *"In the same way, the Spirit helps us in our weakness. We do not know what we ought to pray for, but the Spirit himself intercedes for us through wordless groans."*

GOD IS LIMITED IN HOW HE SPEAKS TO ME

Some people expect God to speak like humans, using an audible voice in their native tongue and body language. Nothing is impossible for God to do. However, God often speaks in more subtle and creative ways. He nudges us through our heart and spirit instead of relying on human forms of communication. We should keep an open mind and expect to hear Him through the various forms that we discussed in Chapter Five, rather than expecting to hear from Him in a set, pre-defined way.

LOW SELF-ESTEEM AND FEAR

Low self-esteem can also make it difficult for us to hear God's voice. A person who has low self-esteem may harbour the belief that they are not good enough to hear from God. Although they are God's masterpiece, fearfully and wonderfully made in God's image, they may believe they are of no value to God. People with low self-esteem often loathe themselves. Their mindset leads them to believe that everyone hates them, including God. As they do not feel comfortable in their own skin, the feelings of anger, frustration and fear within them make it impossible for them to hear and recognise God's voice.

A person with a low self-image is likely to hear a multiplicity of voices in their head bombarding them with messages. Although some of these messages will be positive, they will often filter out the positive messages and focus on the negative ones. The dominant belief is that they are worthless and have nothing useful to give to society.

Rather than tuning into God's voice, people with low self-esteem are vulnerable to deception by the enemy or the voice of Satan. They cannot distinguish between God's voice and other voices. They allow their minds to be bombarded by negative messages such as:

- I am a failure;
- I am stupid;
- I have no talents;
- I am inferior;
- My situation is hopeless;
- God has abandoned me;
- I am powerless and alone; and
- Everyone is better than me.

God would never put such messages in our heart and spirit. When God speaks to us His purpose is to edify and build us so that we can do His work and have a positive impact on others. Unlike the lies from other voices, God's message to us is positive. It makes us feel better about ourselves and draws us closer to Him. It is about possibilities and empowerment. You will receive thoughts such as:

- I am worthy;
- I am precious;
- I have everything I need to fulfil my purpose;
- I am not alone;
- I am loved unconditionally the way I am;
- I am blessed; and
- I should never be afraid – things will work out fine.

A further consequence of low self-esteem is fear. People with low self-esteem do not have the courage to pursue their call and to deal with any challenges that they encounter in the process. They fear taking risks or seizing opportunities in case they fail. They fear success. They fear standing up for their rights. In fact, they are often obsessed with pleasing others at the expense of themselves. They believe if they aim to please others at all times, this will earn their love and respect. Their self-worth is often dependent on external validation from others.

People with low self-esteem are not just in danger of not hearing God's voice. A far greater problem is that they run the risk of missing their call altogether. The problem is that they believe that others are better than them and that God only speaks to people who are blessed with traits that they lack. They sleepwalk through life and live in a state of despair. They are like the servant who buried his talent in the Parable of the Talents in Matthew 25:14-30.

LISTENING TO GOD – SOME PRACTICAL TIPS

Our challenge is to listen attentively and expectantly to God. We were made to have a natural relationship with God like the type of relationship that exists between good parents and their children. We are God's sons and daughters. The problem is not with God. It is with our inability or refusal to listen to what our Heavenly Father is telling us.

There are a number of tips that have helped me over the years to better tune in to God's voice. I will now share these tips with you, but let me first issue a word of caution. We cannot use formulas, rituals, incantations and other mechanical approaches to manipulate God to fulfil our desires or to make Him act differently from how He would otherwise act. The purpose of the tips is to develop our own spiritual resources so that we can become better listeners and disciples. As we gain greater spiritual maturity, we will be better able to hear His voice and act in obedience. Now let us discuss these tips.

PREPARE YOURSELF MENTALLY

Preparation is a necessary step in hearing God's voice. This means you have a positive expectation to hear from God. Take steps to de-clutter your mind so that you can hear God when He speaks. If your mind is too busy with emotions, whether positive or negative, they will drown out God's message. Try and keep your mind in a neutral state and pay attention to what God is revealing to you. Ensure your heart is pure. Rid yourself of feelings of hurt, revenge and the other emotions arising from lack of forgiveness.

PREPARE YOUR PHYSICAL ENVIRONMENT

This is about removing distractions from your environment as far as possible. It is hard to hear God's voice if you are constantly watching television, surfing the internet, busy on your telephone, or too busy chasing wealth and material pleasures. The more you slow down and stay silent, the more effective is your listening. Silence and listening go hand in hand. It is intriguing to note that the letters that spell 'SILENT' are the same letters that spell 'LISTEN'.

We can practice silence wherever we find ourselves. Start by speaking less when you are with others at home, work and elsewhere. I find it helpful to switch the radio off when I drive. When travelling on public transport, it is also a good practice to put the telephone on mute. Find time to practice 'stillness' each day.

- Is your life too busy to hear God's voice?
- Are you one of those people who find it hard to find quality time to spend with God?
- Do you even find it hard to find time for yourself and your family?

He says:

> *"Be still, and know that I am God; I will be exalted*
> *among the nations, I will be exalted in the earth."*
>
> Psalms 46:10

INVEST TIME AND EFFORT IN YOUR RELATIONSHIP WITH GOD
Your relationship with God should be interactive, trusting
and personal. Like all good relationships, you need to invest
time and effort in it to get to know the person well. Each
moment of your life, you should naturally expect to hear
from God. Like your best friend, you should be speaking
to Him about everything that concerns you. Proverbs 3:5–
6 reminds us that we should *"Trust in the Lord with all [our]*
heart and lean not on [our] own understanding. In all [our] ways
[we should] submit to him and he will make your paths straight."

You should not only speak, but you should listen to the
promptings and emotions that are emerging from your
spirit and heart. Listen to your heart for God's guidance and
instructions. God is Love and can be found in your heart, not
in your head. He speaks to our hearts in 'gentle whispers' and
promptings.

We can all learn how to listen from Mary's example. In
Luke 10, we see how Mary chose to listen to Jesus while her
sister, Martha, chose to be distracted by the elaborate meal
she was preparing.

> *"She came to him and asked, 'Lord, don't you care*
> *that my sister has left me to do the work by myself? Tell*

her to help me!' 'Martha, Martha,' the Lord answered, 'you are worried and upset about many things, but few things are needed – or indeed only one. Mary has chosen what is better, and it will not be taken away from her.'" Luke 10: 40–42

God is more interested in our relationship with Him than in what we give to Him.

Young Samuel's example is also instructive. He was able to hear God's voice when he prayed because he was taught by Eli, his spiritual mentor, to listen. He went and lay down to quieten his mind. He then said:

"Speak, Lord, for your servant is listening."
1 Samuel 3:9

Let go of preconceptions about God's voice

God wants to have a relationship with you and He knows that this is built through communication. He is very creative in the way He communicates with us. Don't be rigid in how you expect Him to speak to you. In Chapter Five, we have seen that He communicates with us through a variety of ways. Although He has the power to speak to you audibly, He often speaks to us in more subtle ways through our heart and spirit. Speak to God in the same way you would to a good friend or a close relative. Wait expectantly and listen to what He tells you. Obey whatever instructions you receive from Him.

Remember feedback from Him can come in different forms. Look out for clues in your environment. God may be communicating with you through the people and things that you keep on encountering and noticing around you. Pay attention to your God-inspired thoughts, feelings, desires, the images you notice or the words that enter your mind.

PRAY IN SILENCE

Prayer can help us to hear God's voice. Our prayer will be more effective if it is motivated by a desire to honour God's Will rather than fulfilling our selfish needs. Although we can pray anywhere and anytime, where possible, we should take time to remove distractions from our environment and quieten our minds before we begin to pray. Silence makes it possible to hear what God is saying to us.

Jesus often prayed in silence.

> *"But Jesus often withdrew to lonely places and prayed."*
> Luke 5:16

He started His days with prayer.

> *"And in the morning, rising up a great while before day, he went out, and departed into a solitary place, and there prayed."* Mark 1:35

Ensure that your prayer is not a monologue in which you download all your cares, concerns and the things on your wish-list on God. The goal of our prayer should be to pursue God's agenda. Don't just pray — listen to what God has to tell you. Wait for Him to speak to your heart and spirit. Scottish Theologian, William Barclay, sums it up this way:

> *"Prayer is not a way of making use of God; prayer is a way of offering ourselves to God in order that He should be able to make use of us. It may be that one of our great faults in prayer is that we talk too much and listen too little. When prayer is at its highest, we wait in silence for God's voice to us."*
>
> https://www.quotesdaddy.com/author/
> William+Barclay

We should be prepared to wait for as long as it takes for God to respond to us. As you wait, listen for His voice and obey whatever instructions He gives to you. Good disciples are patient. This is exemplified by the call experience of many of the people called by God that we read about in the Bible. Job had to wait for a long time before his prayers were answered. Abraham and Sarah had to wait for 13 years for God to fulfil His promise to them before their son, Isaac, was born.

FOLLOW A SPIRITUAL DISCERNMENT METHOD

Some people find it helpful to follow a spiritual discernment method. In common parlance, discernment is the ability to judge correctly. Spiritual discernment is about invoking and trusting God to speak to your heart and guide you to see the truth behind every matter or decision you may be faced with in life. It helps us to know the difference between God's voice (the truth) and other voices (false teaching).

A commonly used spiritual discernment method is the one taught by Saint Ignatius Loyola in his *Spiritual Exercises*. The goal of these exercises is to help people to find and know the will of God for their life.

Ignatius discernment principles are based on the premise that there is an inner struggle going on within us and this prevents us from hearing God's voice and following His will. The battle is played out in our hearts and it is one between our 'higher self' and our 'false self'. Compulsive, egotistic and fearful behaviours such as pride, anger, greed, doubt and hate are a sure sign that we are allowing the 'false self' to have the upper hand in our lives. To seek God's Will and hear His voice, we must take conscious steps to:

> *"Therefore, get rid of all moral filth and the evil that is so prevalent and humbly accept the word planted in you, which can save you"*   James 1:21

For an authentic discernment process, Ignatius teaches that we should keep an open mind and heart. We should let go of all preconceptions and attachments. Our goal should be to seek God's Will and respond to Him with obedience and courage. We should resist the temptation to attach conditions to what God may be calling us to do. We should be ready and willing to accept whatever God reveals to us in the discernment process. Courage and trust are needed as God's work often means we have to be prepared to get outside of our comfort zone to do things that we might find to be challenging and risky. If we feel fear, doubt, restlessness and conflicts, Ignatius tells us we should acknowledge these emotions and ask God for guidance and support. Such feelings are a sign of 'spiritual desolation'. They reflect unhealthy attachments and an orientation away from God.

Feelings of love, joy, peace, hope, humility, forgiveness and gratitude, on the other hand, are signs of what Ignatius calls 'spiritual consolation'. They are a sure sign that our relationship with God is healthy, and we are being led and guided by Him.

> *Spiritual desolation moves us away from God while spiritual consolation moves us closer toward God.*

Ignatius also recommends that we should have 'prayerful reflections on our experiences'. He teaches a method of prayer known as *'The Examen of Consciousness'* to help us reflect on our experiences each day. This is about reflecting on the events of our day, the people and circumstances we encountered, and the things we feel grateful for during the day. We should then ask ourselves how God has been present in what we felt and experienced.

By practicing these spiritual exercises daily, Ignatius believed we can more easily tune into God's voice. If you would like to know more about Ignatian spiritual discernment, a useful introduction is Margaret Silf's bestselling book, *The Inner Compass: An Invitation to Ignatian Spirituality* (Chicago: Loyola Press; 2005).

CONCLUDING REMARKS

Many people find it hard to hear God's voice, even though He is constantly speaking to us. Sadly, we place all kinds of barriers in the way and these drown out God's gentle whispers. We are made in God's image and likeness to have a close relationship with Him. Active two-way communication is an essential part of any healthy relationship.

We can live a more meaningful and fulfilling life when we learn to listen to God's voice and obey it. We must also learn to recognise God's voice. A good starting point is to identify the things that are preventing us from hearing God's voice. In this chapter, I have identified a generic list of potential barriers that make it difficult for the average person to hear God's voice. It is probably different for each of us. Do your own stocktake and identify how you can better tune your heart, spirit and mind to hearing from God.

Once you have identified the barriers to hearing His voice, find ways to slow down and remove distractions from your life so that you can have a closer relationship with God. Use the tips and guidance covered in this chapter to seek God's wisdom and guidance as you live out your call on a daily basis. As you become better at hearing God's voice, your life will be transformed. You will receive solutions to your problems. You will grow in confidence as you fulfil your call. Above all, you will enjoy a closer relationship with God and a more fulfilling life.

END OF CHAPTER QUESTIONS

- Can you hear God's voice clearly?
- What kind of distractions do you have in your life?
- Do you recognise God's voice?
- What steps will you take to listen more attentively to God?

Chapter Seven

Calling and Resilience

"He who has a why to live for can bear almost any how."　　　　　　　Friedrich Nietzsche

"And we know that in all things God works for the good of those who love him, who have been called according to his purpose."　　　　　　Romans 8:28

Callings come with tests, challenges and suffering. We cannot achieve what we are called to do within our comfort zone. We will be required to take risks and break down barriers. Life will throw all kinds of curve balls at us and we will need to trust God to guide us through setbacks. In this chapter, I will offer guidance on the type of challenges that we can expect to face during our call and how we can build our resilience skills. I will discuss how God wants us to respond to problems and setbacks. I will also offer tips on how to build your resilience, based on my personal experience.

INTRODUCTION

None of us will sail through our call without difficulties and setbacks. One of the most consistent lessons from people's call stories is that setbacks are inevitable. This is true regardless of who we are. Even Jesus had to endure hardships from the time of His birth until His cruel death. Setbacks can take any number of forms and may arise from different sources. They may be caused by your own mistakes, other factors, or what some would call bad luck. People, for example, fall ill and suffer. Some may become victims of accidents, wars, acts of terrorism and natural disasters.

Joseph's call experience exemplifies the type of challenges that may arise when you are called for service. He was loathed by his brothers. They were jealous of his special gift for interpreting dreams, his fine looks and the special love that his parents had for him. They plotted to kill him. They later changed the plan and sold him into slavery instead. This separated him from his family and the comforts from a wealthy household where he was his parents' favourite. As if this was not enough, his master's wife accused him falsely of sexual harassment and attempted rape. He was sent to prison for a crime he did not carry out. He found himself in an alien environment – a slave and a prisoner in a foreign land. This was far removed from his privileged background.

Joseph's experience bore some parallel with Jesus' life, prompting some scholars to argue that he was an earlier incarnation of Jesus. Like Joseph, Jesus was hated for his greatness. He was sold or handed over to the Romans by one of his disciples. The chief priests and elders plotted to arrest and kill Jesus. Jesus was falsely accused by witnesses before Pilate. He was stripped of his robe, humiliated, tortured and crucified. Like Joseph, Jesus was also exalted after His death.

> *"Therefore God exalted him to the highest place and gave him the name that is above every name"*
> Philippians 2:9

Both were hated for their gifts but were quick to forgive their haters. They both started their ministry at age 30 (*see* Genesis 41:46 and Luke 3:23).

As I explained in an earlier chapter, in my own case, I have experienced more than my fair share of adversities during the course of my call. People have tried to block my call by placing all kinds of obstacles in my way. I have had to confront covert and sometimes overt forms of bullying, harassment and racial discrimination in my quest to secure fair treatment and justice for myself and others. I have suffered insults, humiliations and name-calling. Outside of work, I have also encountered setbacks. These include the death of loved ones, severe ill health, divorce, financial problems, betrayals and other personal disappointments.

You may be wondering, as many have asked over the years – why does God allow people to hurt us during our call? Why does He allow setbacks? Has God abandoned us during our calamities? How can we build our resilience to mitigate the impact of setbacks? The rest of this chapter will address these questions.

YOUR STRUGGLES ARE A PART OF YOUR CALL

What if you could see your problem as something sent by God into your life to equip you for your call? What if you could see the seed of opportunity that is disguised within your problem? Everyone who succeeds in their call experienced problems and setbacks. This is true for people of all generations. In every case, there was a positive purpose behind their problem. Earlier, I mentioned the catalogue of setbacks experienced by Joseph. Joseph later learned that what his adversaries meant for harm, God used for good:

> *"You intended to harm me, but God intended it for good to accomplish what is now being done, the saving of many lives."* Genesis 50:20

If God had allowed Joseph to remain in his comfort zone with his family in Canaan, his family and an entire nation would have perished from a harsh famine. He would not have found himself in Egypt in the presence of Pharaoh where he was able to live out his call – interpreting dreams and offering advice. He would not have become second-in-command to Pharaoh and found himself in charge of his palace and the whole of Egypt. With the power given to him by Pharaoh, he was able to move his entire family to Egypt where they prospered. This was God's reward to him for his obedience in living out his call, in spite of facing multiple setbacks. He rose from being a slave to what we would today term as Prime Minister. After the crisis was over, God led the Israelites out of Egypt back to Israel to fulfil His promise.

Learn to see your difficulties as a part of your call. God has a bigger purpose behind your problems. The problems are harmless on their own. What gives them power to harm us is the way we *respond* or *react* to them. If we look a bit closer at Joseph's experience, we will notice his unflappable faith in God's power to help him overcome his setbacks. At no point in the account throughout the book of Genesis do we read about him blaming God for the injustices he suffered. It was as though he knew implicitly that God had allowed his enemies to test him. He also knew that they could not triumph in the long run. The following quote from Smith Wigglesworth aptly summarises his conviction in God's power and grace.

> *"Great faith is a product of great fights. Great testimonies are the outcome of great tests. Great triumphs can only come out of great trials."* Smith Wigglesworth

Elsewhere in the Old Testament, we read about the trials and setbacks endured by Job. Job's afflictions have been the subject of entire books. By all accounts, he was a very virtuous and prosperous person. Yet God allowed Satan to test him. He ended up losing all his wealth, children, health and status. For seven long years, he maintained his composure and unstinting faith in God. He adopted a positive response in the face of his trials and setbacks, even when his friends ridiculed and mocked him and the God in whom he chose to put his trust.

One of the clearest lessons that we learn from Job's call is that problems are a *test* of our character and our faith in God. In Chapter 1 of Job, there is a conversation between God and Satan about Job. Satan told God that Job's loyalty to Him was conditional. As long as God allowed him to prosper, Satan reasoned that Job would naturally serve God and he would curse Him if God withdraws His blessings from Job. At this point, God *allowed* the devil to test Job.

> *"The Lord said to Satan, "Very well, then, everything he has is in your power, but on the man himself do not lay a finger."*
> Job 1:12

This verse makes clear that nothing can happen to us without God's permission. It also shows that there is a *limit* to what God will allow to happen to us. The phrase *"on the man himself do not lay a finger"* is significant. Even when we lose our health and physical possessions, God ensures we are left with what truly matters – our character, our resourcefulness and the other qualities that define our true self. No one has power over us other than what God allows. God turned from Hezekiah in order to test him and to see what was really in his heart (2 Chronicles 32:31).

The same message is affirmed in the New Testament. Jesus informed Pilate,

> *"You would have no power over me if it were not given to you from above."*   John 19:11

Paul writes:

> *"As Christians, we should expect trials, exult in trials, examine ourselves in trials, and entrust ourselves to God in trials, knowing that they are according to His will"*
>   Hebrews 12:8

God allows adversities to happen because they serve a higher, divine purpose. He could have saved His beloved Son from a cruel death but the bigger purpose behind Jesus' death was more important than Jesus' comfort. We fail to think about God's purpose in the things that happen in our lives and in the world around us. We are socialised to believe that everything in life should be about us and our comfort. We expect to have an abundance of money, material possessions, good health, brilliant children, happy relationships and prosperity in every area of our life. We expect to enjoy these blessings day by day without any interruptions. God is not against us having these things, but He wants us to know that His purpose or will is *greater* than our purpose. First and foremost, it is about Him. It is not about our selfish desires.

God is the Architect of our life. As part of His divine plan,

He has a hand in our fortunes and misfortunes. In all things, He wants us to reflect the image of His Son. Jesus endured His own pain and suffering until the end. At the lowest point of His suffering, He reminded us that what matters is God's Will, not ours.

> *"Father, if you are willing, take this cup from me; yet not my will, but yours be done."*   Luke 22:42

Job eventually learned this very important lesson from his test. In spite of all the dreadful calamities he experienced, he still *worshipped* and *praised* God. He saw the bigger purpose behind his struggles. His response was:

> *"Naked I came from my mother's womb, and naked I will depart. The Lord gave and the Lord has taken away; may the name of the Lord be praised. In all this, Job did not sin by charging God with wrongdoing."*
> Job 1:21

The last sentence in Chapter One of Job is significant: *"In all this, Job did not sin by charging God with wrongdoing."* In today's language, we would say he did not blame God. He did not curse God. He did not lament "why me?" He did not question God's power, knowledge, sovereignty or any of the attributes of God that I discussed in Chapter One. He did not wallow in self-pity.

What a contrast to how we typically respond to problems

in our life. In Chapter One, I touched on the problem of evil in the world and how some people reject God's existence purely on this ground. They argue that an all-powerful, all-knowing, benevolent and forgiving God would not allow evil and suffering in the world. To these people, the existence of wars, earthquakes, hurricanes and other disasters is proof that God either does not exist or does not have the attributes that are ascribed to Him. This thinking is exemplified in Rabbi Kushner's bestseller, *When Bad Things Happen to Good People*. Kushner could not understand why God would allow his son to be born with an incurable genetic disease that killed the teenager after a great deal of suffering. This calamity led the Rabbi to argue that God is not powerful, loving, fair and forgiving.

In his exasperation, Kushner writes:

> *"I believed that I was following God's ways and doing his work. How could this be happening to my family? If God existed, if he was minimally fair, let alone loving and forgiving, how could he do this to me? And even if I could persuade myself that I deserved this punishment for some sin of neglect or pride that I was not aware of, on what grounds did Aaron have to suffer?"*
>
> cited in Ron Rhodes, *Why Bad Things Happen If God is Good?*, Oregon: Harvest House Publishers, 2004, p.62

One wonders what he would have said if his loss was on the same scale as Job's losses. After all, Job lost practically everything apart from his faith in the sovereign, omnipotent and omniscient God. It is interesting to note that God remained present with Job during his suffering and *protected* him. He rewarded him for enduring and passing the test. God did not just restore his fortunes. God went further and multiplied his blessings (*see* Job 42: 12–17). Blessings abounded in the second phase of his life. His wealth doubled. He was blessed with the most beautiful daughters in the land. He was blessed with a long, healthy and joyous life. Above all, his relationship with God became even more solid.

Trials bring blessings. At the end of your problems and trials, you should expect to find yourself better, stronger and more blessed. When next you find yourself with major challenges, embrace them and prepare to be blessed at the end of the process. Don't ask "why me?" And remember that God has not abandoned you during your struggles. He promises to guide and protect you as you face your difficulties with courage and grace.

> *"When you pass through the waters, I will be with you; and when you pass through the rivers, they will not sweep over you. When you walk through the fire, you will not be burned; the flames will not set you ablaze. Do not be afraid, for I am with you…"*
> Isaiah 43:2–5

THE BENEFITS FROM YOUR SETBACKS

> *"Every adversity, every failure, every heartache carries with it the seed of an equal or greater benefit."* Napoleon Hill

I will now look at some of the main benefits from adversity. The benefits from your problems always outweigh the pain and suffering you experience. Here is a list of some of the benefits from enduring personal crises and setbacks.

PREPARATION FOR GROWTH

Your adversity prepares you for growth and to fulfil your destiny. God uses suffering to strengthen us in the same way that a gardener prunes the plants to increase the yield, or a metal worker refines gold in the fire. If teachers did not test children with difficult problems, their intellect would not develop. They would not grow if they were not stretched outside of their comfort zone. Many of us go through life expecting to receive the answer to every question. Would you feel safe flying with a pilot who has never had training to deal with turbulence, adverse weather and other difficult flying conditions? We need to rid ourselves of the unrealistic expectation that everything in life should be smooth and problem-free. If life was without trials, this would not serve us well. We grow and tap more and more into our potential each time we face and overcome a challenge.

Helps you to discover yourself

Adversity is your greatest teacher. It forces you to look within yourself for solutions to your problems. It is only then that you learn about your strengths and your personal capacity to bounce back from difficulties. Adversity forces you to think in new ways and to adapt. Without adversity, many of us would never know about our own personal resourcefulness and the power that lies within us. We emerge from adversities wiser and more emotionally prepared to cope with problems in the future. Charles Spurgeon puts it well when he says: *"Trials teach us what we are; they dig up the soil, and let us see what we are made of."*

Teaches humility

Adversity exposes our vulnerability. It reminds us that we are human and are connected to each other. We suddenly realise that we are not an island. People instinctively turn to each other for support in times of need. We turn to friends, family members, therapists, pets and many of us discover God or improve our relationship with God in times of personal setbacks. It is then that we accept God's promise:

> *"Come to me, all you who are weary and burdened, and I will give you rest."*   Matthew 11:28

Reminds us of the uncertainty of life

Adversity also makes us realise that we should not take anything in life for granted. We can lose our health, wealth, other comforts and even our life in the blink of an eye. All it takes may be a miscalculation, a wrong decision, a senseless act or being in the wrong place at the wrong time.

Think, for instance, of people who leave their homes happy to go on holiday and who get caught up in acts of terrorism. This is what happened in June 2015 when Islamist gunman, Seifeddine Rezgui killed 30 British tourists in the popular resort of Port El Kantaoui, Tunisia.

Promotes perseverance and success

Adversity teaches grit and perseverance. People who succeed in their call keep going in spite of their difficulties. To succeed in any field, you have to keep trying over and over again. A baby learns to walk through constant effort. Researchers found this takes thousands of steps each day and dozens of falls.

Successful people seek to learn from their setbacks. They see their setbacks as an opportunity to learn from their experience. The legendary basket-baller, Michael Jordan, attributes his success to his failures:

> *"I've missed more than 9,000 shots in my career. I've lost almost 300 games. 26 times, I've been trusted to take the game winning shot and missed. I've failed over and over and over again in my life. And that is why I succeed."*

TEACHES GRATITUDE

Adversity often comes with some losses. It may be a financial loss, the loss of your health, a loved one, a job or even your dignity. It may even be the loss of faith in people if your setbacks arise from betrayals or the actions of other people. If we change our perspective, we can see the other side of the coin. Instead of only seeing our losses, we can also see what remains and be grateful for what we have. We can celebrate the fact that we have not lost everything. If we take the time to count our blessings, we may even notice that we are blessed. We may think life has dealt us a bad hand, but we may notice others with bigger challenges than what we face. Imagine, for example, worrying about the loss of a job when your destitute neighbour has no prospect of ever working because of the severity of their mental and physical disability.

BUILDS RESILIENCE

Resilience is the capacity to deal effectively with difficult situations, sadness, loss, stress, failure and setbacks. It is more than coping with difficulties. People who are resilient know how to respond to difficulties, when to seek help, and how to stay physically and mentally strong. They are flexible in their thinking and learn from their experience. They bounce back quicker and stronger than those who lack resilience skills.

Resilience means never giving up, no matter what difficulty you face. I see it as a painful episode which hurts badly but is not final or fatal. Imagine a boxer who is knocked down but not 'knocked out'. He still has the option of getting back up on his feet and have another go. I am reminded of God's promise that we may stumble but not fall.

> *"Though he may stumble, he will not fall, for the LORD upholds him with his hand."*
>
> Psalm 37:24

When handled well, adversity serves to build your resilience and helps you fulfil your call. You may stumble but not fall. Throughout my personal and professional setbacks, I always remain bold and fearless, knowing that I have such a strong promise of protection from my loving and faithful God.

TIPS FOR BUILDING YOUR RESILIENCE

Given the positive role that adversity plays in our life, how can we develop our resilience to better cope with it? Much has been written on this question. As someone who has faced all kinds of obstacles and hurdles during the course of my call, I am well placed to offer some guidance on how to build your resilience skills.

Any guidance on resilience should first recognise our uniqueness. This is one of the messages that runs through each chapter of this book. As unique individuals, this means each of us has our own way of dealing with problems, trials and traumas. What works for one person may not necessarily work for another. Notwithstanding this caveat, almost everyone – if not all – can benefit from the following general guidelines based on my own experience and scores of other people who have overcome major adversities.

CHOOSE AN APPROPRIATE RESPONSE

No matter what setbacks you face or to what depth your life plunges, always remember that you still have the freedom to choose your response to the situation. You can choose to react positively or negatively. You can choose to ride out the storm or let it overwhelm you.

> *"Life is 10% what happens to you and 90% how you react to it."* Charles R. Swindoll

Psychologists tell us that when faced with danger, we are wired to respond in one of three ways – to freeze, flee or fight. If we think of the situation calmly and allow ourselves to be guided, we will know how best to respond in each given situation. We have to know what battles to fight and what battles to do nothing about or flee from.

We also know from the work of psychologists that when we react to adversities with anger, bitterness and other strong emotions, that these emotions are a mere reflection of our *response* to the adverse events or situation. They are not caused by the adverse events. Imagine, for example, two people took a driving test. They both failed and felt different degrees of disappointment. However, after a few days one decides to learn from the experience and to take extra lessons to improve their chance of success next time. The other person, in turn, remains disappointed and decides to give up trying to learn to drive.

Here we see two different outcomes from the *same* adverse event. The different outcomes or consequences come about because of the different *beliefs and behaviours* each person holds about the adverse event. One holds a set of empowering beliefs that they can learn from what happened, and that extra lessons will help them to be successful on the next attempt. The other person holds on to the negative belief that the odds are stacked against them and they will never succeed.

DEVELOP AN EMPOWERING COPING STRATEGY

God gives every one of us a free will so that we can choose beliefs and thoughts that empower us to deal with challenges. If you are struggling to cope well with problems, examine your thoughts and beliefs about the problems you are encountering. Negative and unhealthy thinking styles lead to suffering. Try not to take things personally. If you are faced with a challenging situation, don't blame yourself for it or anyone else for that matter. Accept it for what it is and deal with it calmly and rationally. Take positive actions to deal with it. If you are in debt, for example, take steps to reduce your expenditure and try to find ways of increasing your income. Speak with your creditors and agree a suitable payment plan. Personalising the problem and blaming others will not help you to overcome the debt problem.

REMEMBER THAT PROBLEMS DON'T LAST FOREVER

When we are going through a storm, it is easy to fall into the trap of thinking that it will never end. This is obviously not true. Remember the well-known Persian adage: *"This too shall pass"*. Learn to see your difficulty as a process which you are going through with a start-point and end-point. I find it helpful to see this period as a time to adapt, figure out what lesson I need to learn from the problem, and to prepare to move forward with my call, stronger and better prepared to deal with any future challenges. Try to see your challenges as a 'wake-up call' from God to transform your character and better prepare you for your call. Focus on the benefits, not the pain or suffering.

PUT YOUR DIFFICULTIES INTO PERSPECTIVE

Take time to look at the problem mindfully and rationally. Then ask yourself if what you are going through is the worst thing that could happen to you or to someone. Remember that no matter how bad your situation is, there are people around you who are faced with more horrendous challenges than you. What about the millions of people in the world who are homeless or who struggle daily for food? Are you overreacting? What assumptions are you making about the situation? Is there any evidence to support what you are thinking or feeling? Are you feeling the way you are feeling because you have unknowingly fallen into an unhealthy thinking response to the problem? Ask yourself what is negative and positive about the situation. Then examine your thoughts to see whether you are exaggerating the negatives and minimising the positives.

Think of what you can change

Another helpful tip is to look at the situation objectively. Identify what you can change and what is beyond your control. If something is beyond your control, there is no point in losing time and energy worrying over it. The rational response is to accept it and do what you can to change the things that you can control.

For example, if you are in a relationship that is not serving you, think about your options for changing it. One option is to speak to the other party about how their behaviour affects you. There is also the option of asking a mediator or third party to intervene on your behalf to try to bring about the desired change. A more radical option is to walk away or signal your intention to walk away, although this may not necessarily be the most appropriate response. Sometimes the threat of walking away may be sufficient to effect the desired change. This example illustrates that we do have a choice to change things in many of the difficult situations that life throws at us. We prolong and intensify our suffering when we act powerlessly, as though we are condemned to perpetual misery.

Seek help from others

In times of adversity, it is important to remember that other people can help us to get through it. This depends on your network. Some of us have a large network of family, friends, colleagues and other people who can support us during a crisis. Others live a more sheltered life and have access to fewer people. It is a good idea to build a social network to help prepare you for difficult times. Other people can help by offering different perspectives on your problems. They may also be able to offer moral and practical support.

In my own case, I am blessed to have a large, caring family. We share each other's joy and pain. As a family, we have been through a lot of hardships. I can remember a period of major illness in my life when I lost the use of my left leg, which the doctors could not diagnose. I was in excruciating pain for six months from my left thigh down to my calf. Apart from offering me morphine to control the pain, the doctors were unable to help me. They had exhausted every option and still could not diagnose my condition. I prayed relentlessly and asked God to heal me. Although I had to wait for six months, God answered my prayer and I was miraculously cured. My family was very supportive towards me. Without their practical help, I don't know how I would have got through this difficult period. I knew that God would not abandon me in my time of need and that kept me going. My work colleagues were amazed at the confidence that I showed in spite of the pain and suffering I had endured.

At the time of writing, I have a beloved cousin who is battling for her life. Although she is based in Barbados and some of the family live in the United Kingdom, we stay in contact with her and her mother daily. Knowing that we love and care about her wellbeing helps her to find the strength to keep going, in spite of the debilitating nature of her illness. It also keeps her in a positive state. When we feel positive and confident, we think more clearly and are better able to solve problems.

HAVE FAITH IN GOD

No matter how serious our setback is, God can help us to overcome it. As I pointed out before, nothing can happen to us without God's permission. God cares about us and is with us throughout our problems. We may leave Him but He never abandons us. His plan for us is to edify us and He often transforms us through problems and challenges.

PERSONAL LESSONS ABOUT RESILIENCE

As is clear from what has been said so far, my personal and professional life has been replete with challenges that have served to develop my resilience. It started at the age of 15 when I was forced to get out of my comfort zone in beautiful, sunny Barbados to live in the UK against my will. By age 17, I was married and became separated before my 21st birthday with two young sons aged one and two. This left me emotionally and financially beleaguered.

I did not fare any better in my professional life. God placed me in situations where I could be trusted to carry out my call, notwithstanding the trials and obstacles that I faced in my quest to promote equality of opportunities and justice for vulnerable and socially marginalised groups. I have had to battle against overt and covert forms of institutional racism in organisations that one would expect to be a showcase for love, respect, fairness and justice. It was no easy task, challenging and exposing racist and sexist policies and practices designed to keep minority groups in 'their place'. I found it astounding that some of these organisations even had vested interests in slavery. Slavery may have been legally abolished but negative and stereotypical views of descendants of slaves remain entrenched in many organisations, including some churches. It should be remembered that the church (especially the Anglican and Catholic Churches) played a large role in the transatlantic slave trade and were even owners of slaves and sugar plantations.

Imagine a black woman being called by God to serve as a change agent in this type of organisation. In an ideal world, there would be no need for anyone to have the job roles that I have had. There would no need to have to fight for equality and justice. God created us the same, notwithstanding our uniqueness. We are all born free and equal. Babies and young children know this instinctively. They do not see differences in race, colour, gender, sexual orientation, class, disability, age or any other questionnaire characteristic.

Often my job as a change agent and champion for equality and justice for all felt impossible. However, I learned that so long as you follow your call and remain obedient to God, nothing is impossible. There were times when the job felt like a traveller who has to embark on a long journey at night in foggy conditions on steep, winding and obstacle-laden roads with a poorly maintained car. In spite of the obstacles, I am always guided safely to my destination.

The capacity to achieve such feats against the odds comes from an inner strength and a deep belief in God's love and care for us. I will share some of the ways I went about building my resilience and succeeded against the odds.

LETTERS TO GOD

Research undertaken by psychologists has found that writing about difficult challenges can increase our resilience and improve our health and general wellbeing (*see*, for example, Pennebaker, J., *Writing to Heal: A Guided Journal for Recovering from Trauma and Emotional Upheaval*, California: New Harbinger; 2004). The practice is described in academic literature as 'journaling'. It is a way of distancing yourself from your emotions and reclaiming your power. Although journaling can take different forms, I always find it useful to pour out my feelings and desires in letters to God. I write these letters in the same way as I would write to a loving father. They are very personal and you can share anything and everything. It is safe. No one has access to your thoughts. You also have the assurance that God is aware of your thoughts and will not discard your letters.

Below is an example of a letter which I recently wrote to God during an episode of 'writers' block'.

Dear Heavenly Father God,

I am writing to say Thank You for giving me the breath to start a new day. As you know I am not usually a morning person so I am asking you to give me the strength and comfort to complete the task of writing this chapter for this book. I will honour your request to work as hard as possible. Please help me to be steadfast and not be distracted by all of the obstacles and noises around me. I am asking you to kindly remove anyone or anything that would hinder my progress to my tasks. I know You are the only One who is always here for me. I am relying on you heavily as You alone know my strengths and weaknesses. I pray for my family, friends, community and loved ones locally and globally. Please heal the world and give it peace, and bring about equality and justice for all of your children. Let no one be without justice.

I must hurry now. Thank You for listening. I hope You will have a good day too.

Lots and lots of love

XXX for your Face

XXX for your Feet

Your loving daughter

Dianne

STRENGTH FROM MY FAITH

There is also evidence to show that our faith, beliefs and values can help us through difficult situations. This finding is wholly in line with my personal experience. If you accept

God's omnipotence, omniscience, benevolence and the other attributes discussed in Chapter One, you can be totally fearless in the face of crises and major challenges. God is with us during difficult times. At no time are we alone. We are protected, comforted and guided throughout our trials. So long as we do not allow ourselves to be distracted and we listen to God's voice, we will emerge from our setbacks stronger and better.

Many of the people in the workplace who tried to block and frustrate my call were often baffled by my propensity to succeed against the odds. The more they tried to undermine me, the more strength I garnered for fighting for the cause of justice. Name-calling such as 'loose cannon', bullying techniques such as exclusion from meetings and withholding information that was essential for my work, only served to increase my resolve to secure justice for people seeking sanctuary and other vulnerable groups. I knew that I could call on God to help me and that my back was always covered.

God's Word in Psalm 121 has always played a major role in sustaining me during periods of conflicts and difficulties. It reminds me that my enemies and tormentors are waging a hopeless war. How can they triumph over me with their fragile plans if I am being protected by my Heavenly Father, the all-powerful and living God? If you know and believe with all your heart that your strength comes from the Lord, the Maker of heaven and earth, you can always stand firm in the presence of the unsavoury and malicious people who you will meet at work and in other walks of life. You will live out your calling and let your light shine even brighter the more they try to extinguish it, belittle and distract you from carrying out God's work.

Readers of this book may wish to take a few moments to reflect on what God is saying to them in Psalm 121 (reproduced in the box below). I hope it gives you the same strength and courage that I draw from it.

PSALM 121

I lift up my eyes to the mountains.
Where does my help come from?
My help comes from the Lord,
the Maker of heaven and earth.
He will not let your foot slip.
He who watches over you will not slumber.
Indeed, He who watches over Israel
will neither slumber nor sleep.
The Lord watches over you.
The Lord is your shade at your right hand.
The sun will not harm you by day,
nor the moon by night.
The Lord will keep you from all harm.
He will watch over your life.
The Lord will watch over your coming and going,
both now and forever more.

CARING FOR YOURSELF

In times of turmoil and stress, it is particularly important to look after your personal wellbeing. This is a personal matter and can be done in a variety of ways. Numerous studies have found that regular exercise, healthy eating and adequate sleep are particularly important to increase our capacity to bounce back from adversity.

Exercise does not have to be physically demanding to be beneficial to your health. Any activity that causes your body to work hard enough to increase your heartbeat counts. This could be achieved through brisk walking, swimming, dancing, cycling or even work around the home like cleaning and gardening. In times of crises, I find it therapeutic to go for walks along the beach or in the woods or in open space where I am surrounded by nature. This type of environment helps me to put my personal struggles into perspective. It reminds me that God is greater than my problems and can help me to overcome any situation.

Eating healthily is also important. Some people are tempted to numb their pain with alcohol and substances. This should be resisted at all costs as any relief is at best temporary and will curtail your recovery. Instead, make a conscious effort to eat and live healthily. This includes sleeping and resting adequately, keeping yourself busy with pleasurable activities, learning new skills, taking on new hobbies, going away for short breaks and giving yourself treats. I also find it helpful to listen to inspirational music and reading poetry which reminds me of my inner strength and God's love and majesty. One poem that I have always found to be particularly uplifting is *'Still I Rise'* by Maya Angelou. My other anthem is a song by Labi Siffre – *'Something Inside So Strong'*. This poem and this song remind me of my inner strength and that God can help me to get through any unjust situation or whatever life may throw at me. Observing things in nature also helps to change our perspectives – like watching a bird building a nest, a squirrel scurrying up a tree, the majesty of the moon and stars or the beauty and poise of flowers.

Caring for yourself is also about nurturing a positive self-esteem and self-image. This is certainly not the time to beat yourself up or wallow in self-pity. It is the time to listen to the voice of God and silence your inner critic – the voice in your head that is telling you to blame yourself or others for your problems, to give up because the problem is insurmountable, and you are alone and powerless. Instead, by tuning in to God's merciful and loving voice, you will feel peace in the midst of the storm.

It is important to feel and own your emotions. It is ok to cry. It is also ok to feel shock, anger and disappointment. However, you should make a conscious effort to avoid getting bogged down by these emotions. The quicker you own and accept your problems and challenges, the quicker you can begin to find workable solutions and begin the healing and recovery phase. This is what resilience is all about – bouncing back from heart-wrenching situations and coming out at the other end stronger, wiser and better equipped to deal with even bigger challenges in the future.

Concluding remarks

> *"What, then, shall we say in response to these things? If God is for us, who can be against us?"* Romans 8:31

Nothing can happen to us without God's permission. God did not promise us a problem-free life. This would not be in our best interests. In her book, which addresses the why of suffering, Margaret Clarkson reminds us:

> *"The sovereignty of God is the one impregnable rock to which the suffering human heart must cling. The circumstances surrounding our lives are no accident: they may be the work of evil, but that evil is held firmly within the mighty hand of our sovereign God … All evil is subject to Him, and evil cannot touch His children unless He permits it. God is the Lord of human history and the personal history of every member of his redeemed family."*
>
> Clarkson, Margaret, *Grace Grows Best in Winter: Help for Those Who Must Suffer,* Grand Rapids: W. B. Eerdmans Publishing, 1984), pp 40–41

When faced with a crisis, God expects us to respond in ways that most of us find to be counter-intuitive. We are socialised to expect everything to flow smoothly and to see problems as unnatural and unwelcome. Yet they are one of the principal ways in which God prepares us for our call and to become the persons we were created to be. Like Joseph, Job and other faithful servants in Biblical times, God expects us to face adversities with courage and faith. God commands us to *"be still and know that He is God"* (Psalms 46:1). When you learn to see problems as disguised blessings, you will embrace them with gratitude and composure.

God wants you to pass your tests. With the right response, you can emerge victorious from your trials. Without a stern test, there is no convincing testimony to share with the world. God uses suffering to strengthen us in the same way that a gardener prunes the plants (John 15:2), parents discipline their children (Hebrews 12:10), and a metal worker refines silver and gold in the fire (1 Peter 1:6–7). Psalm 23 teaches us that adversities are 'temporary':

> *"Even though I walk through the darkest valley, I will fear no evil, for you are with me; your rod and your staff, they comfort me."* Psalm 23:4

Note you are passing through the adversity; you are not permanently stuck where you are. Help is also available while you are undergoing your adversity; you are not alone.

Listen to what God is telling you during your trials and respond with obedience, courage and faith. Always remember the *purpose* of your trials and that every cloud in your life has a silver lining. If you focus on the prize that follows, you will have no time to dwell on the obstacles. They are merely the means to the greater end.

END OF CHAPTER QUESTIONS

- What adverse situations have you encountered during your personal or professional life?
- What helped you to cope with these adverse situations?
- What lessons did you learn from your adversities?

Epilogue

Don't Run Away When God Calls

THE JONAH COMPLEX

The key message of this book may be summarised in a few brief sentences. God has created each one of us as a unique expression of His own image and likeness to serve His greater purpose. He lovingly equips us with special gifts and talents that are unique to us so that we can play the role we were created for. Our personality and personal experiences are an extension of the gifts and aptitudes that God endows us with to fulfil our call. Every one of us is a vital and distinct part of the 'whole cosmic machine' and the machine cannot function properly unless each of its parts function and serve its purpose. The world is a poorer place when we fail to show up as our authentic self and live out our calling.

There is nothing more dispiriting than when I see people going through life looking lost and rudderless. At best, these people get by in life, often living for payment to meet their bills. Many find themselves in roles that make little or no use of their innate gifts and talents. We could all flourish and lead fulfilling lives if only we would tune into God's voice and respond to the divine instructions we are given.

There is no need to be jealous of another person's success. They are successful because they are using their God-given talents. You are unsuccessful because you have chosen to bury your God-given talents or sabotage your own growth. It is as simple as that. You allow yourself to be held back by fear and settle for a life of mediocrity. Referring to this fear, Abraham Maslow writes in his very insightful book, *The Farther Reaches of Human Nature*:

> *"We fear our highest possibilities… We are generally afraid to become that which we glimpse in our most perfect moments, under the most perfect conditions, under the conditions of greatest courage. We enjoy and even thrill to godlike possibilities we see in ourselves in such peak moments. And yet we simultaneously shiver with weakness, awe, and fear before these very same possibilities."*

Fear of self-actualisation comes in a myriad of forms. For some of us, this may be:

- fear of failure;
- fear of success;
- fear of responsibility;
- fear of moving outside of our comfort zone; and
- fear of what other people may think of us.

Maslow describes this fear to use our gifts to become the best version of ourselves and to serve others as the 'Jonah Complex'. Remember, God called the prophet Jonah to serve the people of Nineveh. However, Jonah disobeyed the call and fled to Tarshish in a ship where he and the entire crew got caught in a great storm which imperilled their lives. Jonah ended up in the belly of a giant fish for three days as a result of his disobedience. Like many of us, Jonah fled God's call. What a contrast to young Samuel − *"Speak, Lord, for your servant hears"*. Samuel did as he was told, and God gave him his divine assignment.

I hope the call stories discussed in this book will encourage you to think about and find your own calling. What unique contribution have you been placed here to make? What is stopping you from making your distinct contribution? Are you tuned into God's voice or are you listening to other people's false voices − including your own?

Your gifts and talents are useless in the cemetery. God wants you to use them now while you are still alive and are able to be of service to others. It is said that the graveyard is the richest place on earth, given the number of people who die without ever finding and honouring their call. If people like Martin Luther King Jr, Bob Marley, Mary Seacole, Mayo Angelou, Shakespeare or Mozart − to name a few − had died without living out their call there would be no legacy for subsequent generations to enjoy.

My heart floods with joy when I see people fulfilling their call. I smile each time that I see my daughter, Carla, in her element as a lawyer, or my grandson, Tristan, living out his passion as a footballer. They are being paid to do roles that they enjoy and that they would do even if they were not paid to do them. God is also pleased when we do what we were created to do.

I have boldly argued that God is calling every one of us to fulfil our divine assignment. Some people have a problem with this claim. They ask – Is there really a God calling people to perform preordained roles? In Chapter One, I discussed the different perspectives of 'theists' – the believers in God's existence and the 'atheists' and 'agnostics'. Atheists deny the existence of God altogether, while agnostics are sceptical about the existence of God as this is difficult to prove or disprove. This book would be incomplete if I did not present strong, incontrovertible evidence to support my unshakeable conviction in the existence of a merciful, active and sovereign God.

EVIDENCE OF GOD'S EXISTENCE

God's existence does not have to be accepted as an article of faith. It is not something that has to be invented as a figment of our imaginations to explain things that are beyond the grasp of our limited mind. An omnipotent God clearly has the power to return to each of us to prove His existence beyond doubt in ways we can understand. However, there would be no need for faith or even free will. Many of us are like Jesus' doubtful disciples:

"You believe because you have seen me. Blessed are those who believe without seeing me."   John 20:29

For those who need signs of God's existence, new evidence is constantly being uncovered to show that the universe is intelligently designed and is not the result of some random process. Our planet is 'fine-tuned' to support life. As in the *Goldilocks and the Three Bears* children's story, the porridge must be just right – neither too hot nor too cold for life on earth to be possible.

Let us consider a few examples of this fine-tuning of the 'laws of physics'.

THE SIZE AND LOCATION OF EARTH

Earth contains the right mixture of gases to support plant, animal and human life. The distance of the earth from the sun is just right to keep us from freezing or from becoming too hot. The location is also just right to keep water in a liquid state and at the right temperature to sustain life. If it were farther away by even a tiny fraction the water would freeze. If it were closer by even a tiny fraction, the water would be too hot. Each day, the earth rotates around the sun at a constant speed of 67,000 miles per hour, thus allowing the earth's surface to be properly warmed and cooled.

CONSTANT LAWS OF NATURE

The laws of physics that regulate the universe do not change. Gravity remains the same. The earth rotates around the sun in the same 24 hours. Day follows night. The seasons change in the same order. The speed of light remains constant. Dr Warner Von Braun, the architect of the space programme, remarked:

> *"The natural laws of the universe are so precise that we do not have any difficulty building a space ship, sending a person to the moon and we can time the landing with the precision of a fraction of a second."*

There are many other examples of how the laws of physics have been fine-tuned to make life on earth possible. If any of the 'universal constants' of nature were to vary by even a tiny fraction, life on earth would not be possible (*see* McGrath, Alister E., A *Fine-tuned Universe: The Quest for God in Science and Theology*. Louisville, KY: Westminster John Knox Press, 2009).

The hand of God is seen in the order, symmetry and regularity of everything in nature. It is also seen in the shapes, patterns and numbers of every living thing we observe in nature. These include the spiral patterns in shells, seed patterns of sunflowers, leaves around a plant's stem (e.g. the florets of a broccoli plant), the waves formed by water and the design of the ears of most mammals. Take time also to notice the beauty in the other common shapes we find in nature, such as the hexagonal cells formed by bees to hold their honey and the intricate circular design of a spider's web.

Symmetry and mathematical patterns exist almost everywhere we look in nature. The quantum physicist, Paul

Dirac argued that *"God is a mathematician of a very high order and He used advanced mathematics in constructing the universe"* (cited in Flew, pp105–106). Proponents of 'sacred geometry' hold that God created the universe according to a geometric plan. Order, symmetry and beauty are also seen in the way God makes each of us. The writer of the Psalms marvelled at how *"fearfully and wonderfully"* the human body is made:

> *"I will praise thee; for I am fearfully and wonderfully made: marvellous are thy works; and that my soul knoweth right well."* Psalm 139:14

The evidence points in favour of an intelligent designer with the attributes of God, a fact that even die-hard atheists and materialists are beginning to accept. Notable examples of converted atheists include Professor Antony Flew and Professor Frank Tipler. After spending more than 50 years as champion of atheism in a plethora of publications, Professor Flew changed his position in light of the scientific evidence for God. Flew set out his case in a bestselling book: *There is a God: How the world's most notorious atheist changed his mind* (New York, Harper One, 2007). He writes:

> *"Science spotlights three dimensions of nature that point to God. The first is the fact that nature obeys laws. The second is the dimension of life, of intelligently organized and purpose-driven beings, which arose from matter. The third is the very existence of nature."* p88–89

Tipler wrote:

> *"When I began my career as a cosmologist some 20 years ago, I was a convinced atheist. I never in my wildest dreams imagined that one day I would be writing a book purporting to show that the central claims of Judeo-Christian theology are in fact true, that these claims are straightforward deductions of the laws of physics as we now understand them. I have been forced into these conclusions by the inexorable logic of my own special branch of physics."*   Tipler, F.J. 1994. *The Physics of Immortality.* New York, Doubleday, Preface

In a similar vein, remarking on the divine provenance of the laws of nature, John Foster contends that:

> *"The regularities in nature, however you describe them, can be best explained by a Divine Mind. If you accept the fact that there are laws, then something must impose that regularity on the universe. What agent or agents bring this about? ... We shall be rationally warranted in concluding that it is God – the God of the theistic account – who creates the laws by imposing the regularities on the world as regularities."*   cited in Flew, p110

Einstein also made clear his belief in a 'superior mind' at work in the laws of nature. He saw the hand of God in the universe:

"I am not an atheist. I do not know if I can define myself as a pantheist. The problem involved is too vast for our limited minds. ... The human mind, no matter how highly trained, cannot grasp the universe. We are in the position of a little child, entering a huge library whose walls are covered to the ceiling with books in many different tongues. The child knows that someone must have written those books. It does not know who or how. It does not understand the languages in which they are written. The child notes a definite plan in the arrangement of the books, a mysterious order, which it does not comprehend, but only dimly suspects. That, it seems to me, is the attitude of the human mind, even the greatest and most cultured, toward God. We see a universe marvellously arranged, obeying certain laws, but we understand the laws only dimly. Our limited minds cannot grasp the mysterious force that sways the constellations."

Those who continue to deny God's existence tend to rely on the existence of evil in the world to support their arguments, rather than drawing on scientific evidence. The existence of evil in the world does not disprove God's existence or undermine His attributes. God endowed each of us with a free will. The suffering in the world is often the result of how we exercise our free will. God created a universe which the Bible tells us was 'good'.

"And God saw everything that he had made, and behold, it was very good."   cited in Genesis 1:31

The influential physicist, Stephen Hawking, accepted God's existence but put forward an alternative explanation for evil. He held he did *"believe in the existence of God, but that this Divine force established the laws of nature and physics and after that does not enter to control the world"* (cited in Flew, p.xxiii).

There are also those who hold the view that God exists but He does not have the attributes which are given to Him. They argue that an all-powerful, sovereign and benevolent God would not allow suffering in the world. As previously stated, this view is exemplified by Rabbi Kushner. He argues that God exists as a loving God but He is limited in His power. In his own words:

"I believe in God. But I do not believe the same things about Him that I did years ago, when I was growing up or when I was a theological student. I recognize His limitations. He is limited in what He can do by laws of nature and by the evolution of human nature and human moral freedom."

http://www.myjewishlearning.com/article/
when-bad-things-happen-to-good-people/

Kushner's perspective is shared by many. However, they are all missing the point about the role played by suffering and misfortunes in our lives. Suffering is one of God's means for communicating with us.

Kushner's loss pales into insignificance when compared to Job's losses. Yet Job did not question God's existence or power when misfortune struck him. Imagine losing all your wealth, bearing the loss of ten children and finding yourself covered in sores of a leprous nature. That was the position Job found himself in. Yet he remained steadfast in his faith and belief in God's supra-natural powers. Like a refiner's fire, adversities try and test us, purify us, correct our flaws, and strengthen our character. Only then can we truly hear God's voice, trust God and develop the right relationship with God so that we can live life without fear or worry, no matter what circumstances we face. We can find purpose and meaning in difficult times. We can glorify God in such times, not just when things are going well in our lives.

In Chapter One, I discussed God's attributes. God is omnipresent (present everywhere at the same time), omniscient (all-knowing), omnipotent (limitless in power), omnibenevolent (totally kind and generous towards everyone and everything), immutable (unchanging) and sovereign (in control over everything). God is also gracious, merciful, forgiving and patient. It is these qualities that make God – *and God alone* – worthy of our praise and worship. Even when we fail to heed our call, God is forgiving and patient with us.

Staying with Jonah's example, we saw how God commanded the fish to release Jonah unharmed when he prayed to God in his affliction. In the end, Jonah obeyed God's call and went to share God's word with the people of

Nineveh and get them to renounce evil. He finally realised that no one can run from the omnipresent God. Wherever we run or hide, the sovereign and loving God is there.

Now here is the crucial question for you to ponder and answer: Are you prepared to listen and respond with obedience and courage when God calls you to service? Are you prepared to follow young Samuel's example and say *"Speak, Lord, for your servant hears"*. Or are you going to try and flee from God like Jonah?

> *"But Jonah ran away from the Lord and headed for Tarshish. He went down to Joppa, where he found a ship bound for that port. After paying the fare, he went aboard and sailed for Tarshish to flee from the Lord."* Jonah 1:3

References

Angelou, M., *I Know Why the Caged Bird Sings*, New York: Random House; 1969

Barrett, J., *Born Believers: The Science of Children's Religious Belief*, UK: Simon & Schuster; 2012

Behring, K., *The Road to Leadership: Finding a Life of Purpose*, USA: Blackhawk Press; 2013

Clarkson, M., *Grace Grows Best in Winter: Help for Those Who Must Suffer*, Grand Rapids: W. B. Eerdmans Publishing;1984

Flew, A., *There is a God: How the world's most notorious atheist changed his mind*, New York: Harper One; 2007

Frose, P. and Bader, C., *America's Four Gods: What We Say About God – And What That Says About Us*, UK: Oxford University Press; 2015

Hamer, D., *The God Gene: How Faith is Hardwired Into Our Genes*, USA: Anchor Books; 2005

Huggett, J., *Listening to God,* Great Britain: Hodder & Stoughton; 2016

Kushner, H., *When Bad Things Happen to Good People*, USA: Anchor Books; 2004

Lewis, C.S., *The Problem of Pain*, San Francisco: Harper; 2001

Luhrmann, T.M., *When God Talks Back: Understanding the American Evangelical Relationship with God*, New York: Alfred A. Knopf, Inc.; 2012

Maslow, A., *The Farther Reaches of Human Nature*, USA: Penguin Books; 1971

Meyer, J., *How To Hear From God*, London: Hodder & Stoughton Ltd; 2003

McGrath A., *NIV Bible Handbook*, UK: Hodder & Stoughton;2015

Pennebaker, J., *Writing to Heal: A Guided Journal for Recovering from Trauma and Emotional Upheaval*, California: New Harbinger; 2004

Rhodes, R., *Why Bad Things Happen If God is Good?* Oregon: Harvest House Publishers; 2004

Reivich, K. and Shatté, A., *The Resilience Factor: Seven Keys to Finding Your Inner Strength*, USA: Broadway Books; 2003

Rushnell, S., *Divine Alignment: How Godwink Moments guide Your Journey*, USA: Howard Books; 2012

Sentamu, J., *Hope Stories: 20 True Stories Changing Lives Today*, United Kingdom: Darton Longham Todd Ltd; 2014

Silf, M., *The Inner Compass: An Invitation to Ignatian Spirituality*, Chicago: Loyola Press; 2005

Smith, C., *The Wonderful You: Find Your Purpose and Live the Life of your Dreams Now*, Hertford: Hansib Publications Ltd; 2016

Tillich, P. and Braaten, C.E., *A History of Christian Thought*, USA: Touchstone; 1968

Tipler, F.J., *The Physics of Immortality*, New York,:Doubleday; 1994

Tolle, E., *The Power of Now: A Guide to Spiritual Enlightenment*, London: Hodder Paperbacks; 2001

Tomlinson, D., The Bad Christian's Manifesto: Reinventing God, Great Britain: Hodder & Stoughton; 2014

Tutu, D., *God is Not a Christian*, London: Ebury Publishing; 2013

Vanzant, I., *Faith in the Valley: Lessons for Women on the Journey to Peace*, USA: Touchstone; 1996

Walsch, N.D., *Conversations with God – An Uncommon Dialogue, Books 1,* London: Hodder & Stoughton; 1995

Warren, R., *The Purpose Driven Life: What On Earth Am I Here For?* Michigan: Zondervan; 2002

INTERNET SOURCES

http://www.arrestrecords.com/15-surprising-ex-convicts-who-made-it-big/

http://www.ignatianspirituality.com/making-good-decisions/an-approach-to-good-choices/an-ignatian-framework-for-making-a-decision

http://www.myjewishlearning.com/article/when-bad-things-happen-to-good-people

http://questgaycatholic.org.uk/about/

https://www.quotesdaddy.com/author/William+Barclay

http://religion.blogs.cnn.com/2012/12/29/my-take-if-you-hear-god-speak-audibly-you-usually-arent-crazy/

https://www.stevepavlina.com/blog/2005/01/how-to-discover-your-life-purpose-in-about-20-minutes/

Blank Pages for Notes and Reflections